IT'S MORNING AGAIN IN AMERICA

It's Morning Again In America

President Donald J. Trump & The Movement to Make America Great Again!

Judge Hal Moroz

NEW YORK   ATLANTA   RICHMOND   WASHINGTON

It's Morning Again in America
President Donald J. Trump &
The Movement to Make America Great Again!

Judge Hal Moroz

Access to the vast public records and writings contained in this book
Is available through a wide range of sources in the public domain.
The author of this work wishes to acknowledge the Library of Congress, the National Archives, the Smithsonian Institution, the U.S. Senate, and the exceptionally outstanding archives of The Ronald Reagan Presidential Foundation located in Simi Valley, California.
The author is a member of the Foundation, and encourages everyone interested in supporting and preserving the legacy of President Ronald Reagan to join the Foundation.
Membership can be obtained by writing The Ronald Reagan Presidential Foundation,
40 Presidential Drive, Simi Valley, California 93065, or via the internet at
http://www.reaganfoundation.org

Unless otherwise noted, Scripture quotations are from
The King James Version of the Bible.

The opinions expressed in this book are solely the opinions of the author and do not necessarily reflect the opinions of any individual, groups,
organizations or business entities mentioned herein.
The quotes, selected writings, and articles contained in this book are reprinted with permission or are permissible for use under existing law.

Printed in the United States of America

When America is united, America is totally unstoppable!

There should be no fear! We are protected, and we will always be protected! We will be protected by the great men and women of our military and law enforcement and, most importantly, we are protected by God!

Now arrives the hour of action! Do not let anyone tell you it cannot be done! No challenge can match the heart and fight and spirit of America! We will not fail! Our country will thrive and prosper again!

Together, We will make America strong again! We will make wealthy again! We will make America proud again! We will make America safe again! And yes, together, we will make America great again!

Thank you! God bless you! And God bless America!

~ President Donald J. Trump,
January 20, 2017

All to the Glory of God

It's Morning Again In America

Contents

[Pictures of and with Judge Hal Moroz, pages 110 – 118]

Introduction

Our Hour of Action

Freedom is never more than one generation away from extinction. We didn't pass it to our children in the bloodstream. It must be fought for, protected, and handed on for them to do the same, or one day we will spend our sunset years telling our children and our children's children what it was once like in the United States where men were free.

~ President Ronald Reagan

America dodged a bullet on November 8, 2016!

However, we are a nation on life support. The damage inflicted upon our core institutions, our Constitution, and our Founding Principles was immense. In a mere eight years, America suffered the swift and catastrophic erosion of the very pillars of the republic. And this is no exaggeration. ObamaCare, illegal immigration, Islamic terrorism, anti-Christian bigotry, sanctuary cities, voter fraud, and the death of our Constitutional system of checks and balances are the evidence of our flirtation with extinction as a shining city on a hill and the last best hope for man on earth.

Our present condition is much worse than the one we faced in 1981 as a result of the Carter Legacy. I remember those days.

The election and swearing in of Donald Trump would suggest the dawn of a new era for America. We have ended the disastrous presidency of Barack Hussein Obama, and we now look forward to a new day. It's Morning Again in America!

But America faces many challenges. Our domestic troubles are many, and on the international front we face a relentless enemy, not Communism or Nazism as in the past, but with a renewed and re-invigorated enemy of civilization as we know it. And that enemy is Islam. By its own stated "holy book," Islam is incompatibility with the Civilized World, and its ongoing campaign to exterminate any and all beliefs other than its own, is evidence of this fact. Islam is a self-declared existential threat to the United States and our American way of life. But we as a government have chosen to ignore this threat at our own peril, and this time of peace and prosperity, dubbed "Pax Americana" by historians, is quickly ebbing away. Action is required to meet the challenges we face and ultimately preserve the republic.

It deserves noting that before Pax Americana, there was Pax Britannica, and it was said of Britain that "the sun never set on the British empire." It was vast and stood for centuries. It was the product of a combined naval and land military might that enabled the British to economically prosper. Great Britain ruled the waves, but the sun did finally set on that empire.

America's time of peace and vast economic, political, and military success are similar to Pax Romana. Rome enjoyed centuries of economic expansion, territorial acquisition, and military superiority. Rome, like America, still had wars, but they were limited and did not impede the growth of the superpower. Indeed, it can be said of both Rome and America that with their ascendency civilization prospered. Manufacturing, trade, agriculture ~ all expanded without interruption, to heights that were unachieved by any nation before.

But, alas, Pax Romana was no more. It was ended from within and without. After a long history of achieving peace through strength, Rome began to lose wars and territories. Barbarians entered its gates and changed its culture. Its armies defeated, its cities ransacked, and its heart stopped. But this death was not without its warning signs. And the greater tragedy was that Rome's demise ushered in the Dark Ages for the entire world.

America is at such a point in history. But in true American fashion, We the People united in 2016 under the banner of a Movement to change the course of American history in, and that Movement was led by a brash New York businessman by the name of Donald J. Trump.

We the People constitutionally elected change in 2016, and that change was personified at noon on January 20, 2017, with the swearing in of Donald J. Trump as the 45th President of the United States of America.

In the perception of the mainstream media, President Trump stands alone. He lacks the support of the media, the Congress, the Judiciary, and many in the political party he has identified with. President Trump's only ally is a popular movement of We the People, everyday citizens of the country who had enough of politics as usual, and rose up to stand in the gap for America.

These are historic times we live in! America has never had a President like Donald Trump, or a time as precarious as the one in which we now live.

There is in fact a silent coup underway in America. Democrats in Congress are openly calling for the impeachment of President Trump. Liberal insurgents in our federal judiciary have substituted their will for the Law. And a well-entrenched Liberal Establishment in our intelligence apparatus, spurred on by the arguably unconstitutional acts of the previous Obama regime, is bent on sabotaging the Trump agenda and finally pushing America into the ashbin of history's fallen superpowers. We cannot allow this to happen!

Let me cut to the chase and make this perfectly clear: If the extent of our involvement in the Movement to Make America Great Again was only to elect Donald Trump President, then America is doomed!

Even now, the Deputy Chair of the Democratic National Committee has called for the "Impeachment" of President Trump.[1] Other Democrat operatives have joined in the chorus as well. And if the Republican Party should lose its slim majority in the House of Representatives and the Senate in the 2018 midterm elections, that wishful thinking on the part of the Liberal Establishment could become a reality. We cannot allow this to happen!

---

[1] Minnesota Democrat & Muslim Rep. Keith Ellison, February 22, 2017.

President Trump has a 2-year window of opportunity to substantially purge the illegals currently registered to vote, with California being the largest culprit. He must also deliver on his many campaign promises, not the least of which include deporting illegal criminals and building a great wall across our southern border with Mexico.

Even with our continued support of President Trump and the Movement to Make America Great Again, huge questions remain. And those questions are: Is it too late to truly Make America Great Again? Is America at the point of no return? That is, Has America crossed the Rubicon? Are we on the verge of another Dark Age in the history of the world? Is there still time to actually change the course of America's history? What needs to be done? And, what can we do?

It's Morning Again in America answers these questions ... and more!

This work shines a light. It is a book of many chapters, all of which point in one direction: Toward building a better America and making her great again! Some chapters are long, others short. I share facts and stories in a series of essays. They make a point and move on. Some are not as obvious as others. They form a one-two punch, story and substance, to make a point, all in the bright light of reason. And students of mine know me for teaching to a standard, not to time. In other words, say what you have to say, and do what must be done, then move on. This book is no different. Length does not necessarily connote learning, significance, or a positive outcome. And I am often reminded of other documents in the history of man. Here are a few. You rank their significance:

- Pythagorean theorem: 24 words.
- Archimedes' Principle: 67 words.

- The Lord's prayer: 74 words.
- The 10 Commandments: 179 words.
- The Gettysburg address: 286 words.
- The Declaration of Independence: 1,300 words.
- U.S. Government regulations on the sale of cabbage (circa 1990): 26,911 words.

Benjamin Franklin, one of our Founding Fathers, was both a prolific writer and great thinker. His signature appears on both the Declaration of Independence and the Constitution. He often posed questions in his many commentaries. He then went on to answer those very same questions.

"How shall we judge the goodness of writing?" Franklin once wrote, and went on to answer, "To be good it ought to have a tendency to benefit the reader, by improving his virtue or his knowledge."

It is my sincere hope that this book will be received as a good book, that is, a writing that will benefit its readers in a small but meaningful way. Ideally, this work will improve the knowledge and virtue of its readers, and motivate men and women of good will to take up the banner of making America great again, and take part in the electoral process. As I said, this book is a vision. And, as did the ghosts to Scrooge in the immortal Dickens Classic, *A Christmas Carol*, I have attempted to provide a glimpse of the past, a look at the present, and a vision of the future. Whether or not the shadowy events I foretell come to pass is a matter of destiny, and that destiny lies in the hands of Divine Providence and We the People. I hope we choose wisely — trusting in God, believing in ourselves, and daring to dream great thoughts for our country! Our duty demands nothing less, and our posterity deserves nothing more.

"The ancient Roman and Greek orators could only speak to the number of citizens capable of being assembled within the reach of their voice," Franklin wrote, "their writings had little effect, because the bulk of the people could not read. Now by the press we can speak to nations; and good books, and well-written pamphlets, have great and general influence."

What was true in 1776 remains true today. Good books speak to nations and greatly influence their citizenry. Let this book speak to a great Nation, and influence a great and good people.

It's Morning Again in America!

Fill the cup, sound the fife, one hour of glorious life is worth an age without a name.

~ Sir Walter Raleigh

With all the creative energy at our command, let us renew our faith and our hope. We have every right to dream heroic dreams. Let's make America great again!

~ President Ronald Reagan

Chapter 1

The Great Re-Discovery

But I never thought it was my style or the words I used that made a difference: it was the content. I wasn't a great communicator, but I communicated great things, and they didn't spring full bloom from my brow, they came from the heart of a great nation--from our experience, our wisdom, and our belief in the principles that have guided us for two centuries. They called it the Reagan Revolution. Well, I'll accept that, but for me it always seemed more like The Great Re-Discovery, a re-discovery of our values and our common sense.

~ President Ronald Reagan
Farewell Address, January 11, 1989

"This is a Movement," my wife said. "It's the kind of thing that changes everything!"

It sent a chill through me, because I felt it too!

"And," she said, "I've had this feeling for a while that you are part of it!"

It was a recognition that a battle was on, a battle between two distinct and incompatible ideologies. One rooted in the Christian ethic that founded this great nation, and the other in a political philosophy masquerading as, what President Obama called, "A religion of peace." That so-called "religion" was emerging again from the ashbin of the Dark Ages. It was powerful back then, but was blunted and isolated by the Crusades, a great force for good that ended the Dark Ages. But we are once again engaged in a battle between the forces of good and evil!

I knew something big was going on. I had seen it before. It involved average Americans, and it happened in 1980. I know, because I was a participant in it!

Then, like now, the country was floundering ... failing, to be more precise. We had a failed presidency back then. Jimmy Carter campaigned with the slogan, "Once and for all, why not the best?" But he turned out to be an intellectual from Georgia with a glaring inability to conduct foreign affairs. He gutted the military and our intelligence communities, and appeared incapable or utterly incapacitated by a third world Muslim dictatorship that was holding American hostages and daring us to attack. America's morale seemed never lower, even when we walked away from the War in Vietnam, leaving the families of 55,000 dead servicemen wondering was it all worth it.

We again live in the wake of a failed presidency. A man with no discernable leadership experience with a dubious background promised "Hope and Change!" The "Change" was nothing less than the transformation of America from a world power, with a world class healthcare system and a magnificent military force, to a nation haphazardly fumbling through foreign affairs and again staring helplessly at the same third world Muslim dictatorship that again held American hostages, and again daring us to attack them and shouting "Death to America!"

Now, as before, there is a "Movement" afoot, an invariable Revolution! But back then it was led by a former actor and two-term governor of California, Ronald Reagan. He inspired the Reagan Revolution! With a campaign slogan of "Let's Make America Great Again," Reagan ushered in a coalition of the young and old, rich and poor, North and South, Republican and Democrat, to coalesce around the proposition that the Founding Principles of this nation could be restored.

In many ways, Jimmy Carter set the stage for a Ronald Reagan Presidency. Americans were sick and tired of Carter, who led America's impotence in the post-Vietnam era. Even the Republican Party at the time was controlled by the Rockefeller Establishment, and did not appreciate the prospects of an "outsider" like Reagan changing the status quo. That GOP "establishment" was pro-tax, pro-abortion, and went along with the liberal Democrat agenda of reckless tax and spend policies. And they failed to act in the face of unprecedented cuts in America's military and intelligence-gathering communities.

But Reagan changed all that. He led a great coalition to make the Republican Party the party of lower taxes, pro-life, and national defense! He drew the line on Communist expansion, and acted when countries like Cuba and the Soviet Union dared cross that line in places like Grenada! Reagan let Islam war against itself, and that was nowhere more apparent than on the Iran-Iraq border, where both sides lost millions of jihadists in a cultural war. The GOP became the Party of Reagan, and America and the West were better for it!

Reagan stood for a bold vision of America as that shining city on a hill. He was an unapologetic Christian who opposed abortion and big government. Reagan believed in peace through strength, holding to the notion that America's best approach for keeping the peace was through a superior military force that had a commander in chief with the resolve to protect America's national interests at home and abroad.

Reagan also understood that that military force could not be achieved and maintained without an economically strong engine that outfitted and equipped that juggernaut. Reagan reduced the regulatory burdens on the private sector, reduced taxes and government waste, rebuilt America's military, and renewed the great American Spirit! It was an historic period! I should know. I was there!

And once again today, "There is a Movement here," to quote Donald J. Trump when he was a candidate. This Movement is again designed to stop America's decline in the face of a Democrat President's failed policies, and again free America and the GOP from the grips of an entrenched establishment.

And if those similarities were not enough, it deserves noting this Revolution is also led by a political outsider, Donald J. Trump, who suffers from much of the same ridicule endured by Ronald Reagan. Perhaps even more!

Not since Ronald Reagan have we had a President so poised to change America for the better as we do with Donald J. Trump. A successful billionaire businessman with a bold vision for America, President Trump demonstrates a bravado and can-do spirit that is alien to our political realm. It is a refreshing, no-nonsense brand of American Exceptionalism personified. President Donald J. Trump is the man of the hour to captain this revolution, and like Reagan, he was once a Democrat. And like before, I am once again in the midst of this revolution, taking sides and standing in the gap for America!

But it deserves noting that as rich and powerful as Donald J. Trump is, his wealth and power fade in comparison to the strength of his message, and that message is the path to making America great again! And it is a message that must endure and outlive this president's administration if America is to survive and prosper. This fact must be made clear, or my efforts to raise awareness and produce a call to action are in vain.

As President Reagan forewarned in his Farewell Address,

> "Finally, there is a great tradition of warnings in Presidential farewells, and I've got one that's been on my mind for some time. But oddly enough it starts with one of the things I'm proudest of in the past 8 years: the resurgence of national pride that I called the new patriotism. This national feeling is good, but it won't count for much, and it won't last unless it's grounded in thoughtfulness and knowledge...Our spirit is back, but we haven't reinstitutionalized it."

President Reagan was right! Our great American spirit burned bright in those days. It was Morning Again in America! But the morning quickly dissipated in the malaise and despicable years of the Clinton Administration, and has since become twilight's last gleaming for America with the fruition of the socialist, anti-Christian agenda of the Obama era.

In so many ways, America is like the Alamo, under siege and waiting on that remnant of America that still believes in our Constitution and our Founding Principles to come to the aid of the republic in this her hour of need ... before it is too late! You and I can do that!

But this is not a story about me ... it is a story about America! It is a story and a recipe to support the Movement and the Administration of President Donald J. Trump to Make

America Great Again! It's Morning Again in America!

I stand by the proposition that America is now a declining world power! Morally, militarily, economically, and structurally, America is collapsing. The American "peace" is over!

America's decline as a world power has accelerated most in the second term of Barack Hussein Obama. As he promised Russia's President during his campaign for a second term,[2] Obama's re-election freed him from the shackles of being accountable to the American people.

To his credit, Obama kept his word to the Communist leader. He tacitly stood by as Russia seized vast portions of the globe. From the Ukraine to Syria, Russia moved militarily without anything more than verbal opposition from the Obama regime.

Moreover, Obama was better than his word to Russia. He relieved the Kremlin from further subsidizing the bankrupt Castro dictatorship on the island of Cuba by restoring

---

[2] On March 26, 2012, President Obama was inadvertently recorded on an open microphone telling Russian President Dmitry Medvedev the following:

"Yeah, I understand. I understand your message about space," President Medvedev replied. "Space for you…"

"This is my last election," Obama observed. "After my election I have more flexibility."

"I understand," responded Medvedev. "I will transmit this information to Vladimir."

diplomatic relations with the Communist government and offering lucrative economic benefits to its failed economy.

While the world had experienced a seemingly miraculous collapse of global Communism in the wake of the Reagan Administration, Obama breathed new life into the dying dictatorships. And this transfer of America's mantle of power was also realized in the Islamic world ...

Obama began his promotion of Islam's ascendency on the world scene by declaring it "a religion of peace," and further vowed to "never be at war this Islam!" He then went on to lambast one of the very few remaining Arab countries in the Middle East (Syria) that protected the free exercise of the Christian faith within its borders, and opted to finance and arm Muslim fundamentalist insurgents that, in addition to seeking to topple the Syrian regime, routinely beheaded and crucified Christians in the lands they overran and occupied. These Obama-backed Muslim barbarians also took to destroying any vestiges of monuments that stood as Christian or Jewish holy sites and reminders to the region's rich Judeo-Christian history. And this damage is not being contained.

Obama was joined by his Secretary of State, John Kerry, in orchestrating a complete reversal of the sanctions and effective containment of militant Islam with a treaty favoring Iran that they masqueraded as an Executive "Deal." Unopposed by the Republican leadership of Speaker John Boehner and Senate Majority Leader Mitch McConnell in the Congress, Obama brazenly offered the mullahs in Iran [and the world's leading sponsor of terrorism] $150 billion, the lifting of decades-old sanctions, and U.S. nuclear technology to fuel their radical agenda. Even in the face of repeated chants of "Death to America" and promises to "drive the Jews into the sea" and effectively end the State of Israel, Obama moved ahead with his unconstitutional "Deal" and repeatedly shunned the State of Israel, going so far as to boycott Israeli Prime Minister Benjamin Netanyahu's historic addresses to the United States Congress and the United Nations in 2015 AND orchestrate an international attack on Israel in the UN the following year.

Treaties under the Constitution require a two-thirds approval vote in the U.S. Senate. But not trusting the Constitution, Obama labeled the treaty with Iran an Executive "Deal," and in so doing circumvented the possibility of a defeat in the Senate by gaming the system to disapprove the "Deal," if they chose. That would force a Veto by Obama, which would require a two-thirds vote in the Senate to override the veto. The Republicans simply did not have a sufficient majority to override, thus ceding the high ground to Obama and the Democrats.

This "Deal," Obama alleged, was our last hope to stop Iran from building and using a nuclear bomb. The utter absurdity of that position was the notion that the world's number one sponsor of terrorism would do nothing with the $150 billion windfall provided by Obama. I would argue Iran could do much more damage with the $150 billion disbursed to anti-American interests around the globe. When you consider what less than two dozen Muslims did on 9-11 without a nuclear bomb or massive funding, the prospects of what they can do with $150 billion is staggering!

Iran's argument for the "Deal," which was supported by the Obama administration, was that Iran needed nuclear technology to provide for its energy needs. Another preposterous proposition! Iran sits on vast deposits of oil, enough to provide for its energy needs for the next millennium. And I find it a bit more than curious that an administration like Obama's that is supposedly so sensitive to "climate change" and the "dangers posed by nuclear power" would be so quick to support the Iranian Muslims in advancing their nuclear programs.

In addition to the unconstitutional windfall Obama provided Iran on its economic and nuclear technology fronts, huge inventories of American logistical assets were handed over to the Iranians and their brethren in support of their occupation of territories previous paid for by the blood, sweat, and lives of America's sons and daughters on the battlefields of Iraq. It is a wholesale capitulation to the Muslims of Iran and the ISIS savages, who have effectively extinguished the last remnant of Christendom in those regions of the Middle East. Indeed, a new and more ominous Muslim Dark Age has descended upon the Holy Lands.

To add insult to injury, Obama opened the gates of this once shining city on a hill to Muslim jihadists posing as "refugees," and he did so without opposition from the Republican-led Congress. These "refugees," young men of military service-age, have already destroyed vast areas in the Middle East, and wreaked havoc in Europe. They now seek to head for an American city near you and me, that is, unless Congress summons up enough courage to support President Trump and stop this wholesale undermining of our country and its civilization!

This State of our Union and Western Civilization is the overriding theme of this book. I submit that this is, as President Trump said, "Our hour of action," a time of bold action, an awakening of the once "Silent Majority" that President Nixon spoke of, to once again renew the promise of America in this, our third century as a nation.

Times have changed since the '80s, and so have I. In the most personal of ways, I am a new creature, but my love of country and firm belief in the righteousness of the Conservative movement and the Reagan Revolution it spawned remains. In many ways it is stronger than ever!

And in the finally analysis, this is a book about America! It is, I pray, a call to action, and a source of hope and encouragement.

It's Morning Again in America!

In the pages that follow are timeless truths, and documented successes and setbacks in the many skirmishes in this war for the hearts and minds of our fellow-countrymen. They point the way to a better future, but that future is far from being secured, for the work is far from being done. We must reclaim the surrendered ground to win this war.

The time is now for a re-awakening of the American Spirit, and a re-discovery of the America envisioned by our Founding Fathers and President Reagan. This is why I wrote this book, and so many other books, including *America at Sunset* and *Re-Discovering Ronald Reagan* in 2014, a compilation of our 40th President's major speeches -- a blueprint, if you will -- on how we might preserve, protect, and defend this "last best hope for man on earth" and make America great again!

The bottom line is this: The time is now for American men and women of courage and good will to stand in the gap for our country as never before. The stakes are that high. America is on the brink. But we now have genuine leadership in the White House, and President Trump has a plan to Make America Great Again! Let it be said of us that we mastered our moment, that we held tight to the reigns of our destiny, and we refused to settle for anything less than what was best for America. We can do that! Let it be said that in what would have been the final days of our republic, we changed the course of American history! "And, after all," as President Reagan said in his first inaugural address, "why shouldn't we believe that? We are Americans!"

It's Morning Again in America!

We need you. We need your youth. We need your strength. We need your idealism to help us make right that which is wrong. Each generation goes further than the generation preceding it because it stands on the shoulders of that generation. You will have opportunities beyond anything we've ever known.

~ President Ronald Reagan, May 17, 1981

Chapter 2

A Republic, If You Can Keep It

We have been assured, sir, in the sacred writings, that 'except the Lord build the house they labor in vain that build it.' I firmly believe this; and I also believe that without His concurring aid we shall succeed in this political building no better than the builders of Babel; we shall be divided by our little partial, local interests, our projects will be confounded and we ourselves shall become a reproach and a byword down to future ages. And, what is worse, mankind may hereafter, from this unfortunate instance, despair of establishing government by human wisdom and leave it to chance, war, or conquest.

Only a virtuous people are capable of freedom. As nations become more corrupt and vicious, they have more need of masters.

~ Benjamin Franklin

At the conclusion of America's Constitutional Convention of 1787, as the delegates exited Independence Hall, an anxious crowd gathered, wondering what the Founders had envisioned for the fledgling United States of America. A prominent socialite of the day, a Mrs. Powel of Philadelphia, caught the attention of Benjamin Franklin and asked, "Well, Doctor, what have we got, a republic or a monarchy?" Without hesitation, Franklin answered, "A republic, if you can keep it."

The question of whether or not this Republic can endure has been posed many times by many sources, but none so often and by as many as today. The Civil War, the assassination of several presidents, the scandals of yesteryear, Vietnam ~ all pale in comparison to the challenges we now face in preserving this "last best hope for man on earth," as President Reagan called her.

I spoke about this moment in history on a radio talk show hosted by my friend, Von Goodwin, in July of 2015. I shared my thoughts and views on the state of the union, and Von suggested my views, which were consistent with the birth of America, seemed somewhat prosaic and out of the mainstream. He nevertheless suggested that these ideas needed attention perhaps more now than ever before in our history as a republic. After much thought, I agree.

And it is interesting to note that during that on-air radio conversation, I was asked to comment on my idea of the candidate best poised to win the presidency in 2016. Without hesitation, I responded, "Donald Trump!" I believe Von was less convinced of the sincerity of Donald Trump to follow through in his campaign. I thought otherwise, along with a select few individuals outside the inner sanctum of the Trump campaign, author and patriot extraordinaire Ann Coulter being another, as was radio host Audrey Russo. Ann and Audrey touted Trump's successful potential from the start, and we became mutual followers of each other on Twitter since that time.

You could say my idea for writing this book came amidst the 2016 presidential election campaign. Its predecessor was *America at Sunset: The End of Pax Americana*, which was my effort to convince fellow Americans to elect bold Conservative leadership for our republic, Donald Trump in particular. I was honored to have then-candidate Donald Trump, under his Twitter ID of @realDonaldTrump, Re-Tweet my comments on his campaign on numerous occasions. And many in his campaign followed me on Twitter as well.

Philosophically, I am a Conservative and I have historically voted for the most Conservative Republican in every election since 1976, when I cast my first vote for Ronald Reagan to defeat a sitting incumbent president, Gerald R Ford. Donald Trump's positions on American Exceptionalism, a great wall along our southern border with Mexico, his support for the military, our veterans, law enforcement and Christendom made him the ideal candidate.

But even with the follow through and election of Donald Trump as our 45th President, we are at a crossroads in America! One road leads to a continued republic, and the other to a dictatorship. The choice of which path we follow is still ours, but we are certainly running out of time to make that decision on our own. We stand at a precipice. America, for a variety of reasons we shall address, has been weakened at home and abroad, perhaps a better word would be crippled. The power America once projected as a moral leader and proponent for good around the globe appears to have come to an end. The sun is setting on this shining city on a hill. The light we once projected has dimmed, and at risk of going out.

President Reagan was my ideal of a statesman and American patriot. He embodied the Founding Principles I had come to embrace and articulate in my own life. His philosophy was simple: American government was based on our founding document, the Constitution. This meant government had limited powers, which were enunciated in that founding document, such as, providing for the common defense.

President Reagan understood that the primary responsibility of the government was to provide for the safety of its citizens. This is why we have a standing army, secured borders, local police and firefighters, and the Constitution itself. Out of this controlling principle, the federal government had its responsibilities and the states had theirs. Whatever was not the dominion of the federal government as articulated in the Constitution was reserved to the states and we the people. This embodies the principle of federalism, which is codified in the 10th amendment to the Constitution.

However, today, some 40-plus years after I first voted, that philosophy of limited government and the notion that Americans could control their own destiny is lost. We now find the vast majority of Americans have lost faith with a system that they rightly feel has betrayed them.

In the past few years, America has gone through a radical transformation. This is no exaggeration. Who can honestly say we are better off today than we were a decade ago? Rising taxes, a weakened and demoralized military, American embassies sacked and our Ambassador killed [for the first time since the Carter Administration], the finest healthcare system in the world being dismantled to fulfill the dream of a socialist in the White House and his allies in the Congress, illegal immigrants running unchecked across our borders and corrupting our culture, America's standing in the world diminished, and the list goes on and on.

President Trump can only do so much. It will take a Conservative-Republican Congress to follow his lead, and a Judiciary that strictly interprets the Constitution. In this respect, the Movement to Make America Great Again must be more than just a passing fad. It must be nurtured and preserved by the election of Conservative-Republicans to both houses of Congress in 2018 and beyond!

At a time in our history when the great and noble deeds of our last generation freed a world from the tyranny of communism, we find a new emergence of that bankrupt philosophy in the very seat of our national government, with Chuck Schumer and Nancy Pelosi now leading the charge … with their obstruction to positive change! And there are many on the sidelines preparing to carry that corrupt banner, amongst whom we find the Democrat Party and their allies in the mainstream media and the judiciary.

Would my father, who died a month before the assassination of President Kennedy in 1963, even recognize the America of today if he were alive? Or for that matter, does the America of today even resemble the America that existed during the administration of President Reagan? Sadly, I think not to both. We are not better off than we were ten, or thirty, or 100 years ago for that matter. Today there are more Americans on welfare than there are fulltime employed. The Democrats have effectively tipped the scales in the electoral process to their dependents in this new age welfare state. And now they seek to remove any requirement for voters to positively identify themselves, effectively opening the door to voter fraud and giving illegal immigrants the right to vote.

Despite the best efforts of President Reagan and those of us who proudly participated in the Reagan Revolution, Americans have turned their backs on the core principles which made us a great nation. We failed to institutionalize the Conservative changes of the Reagan Revolution, and their popularity waned. Led by Obama and his cohorts, the Liberal Establishment and their champions in the Judiciary and the mainstream media, quietly dismantled our foundational pillars. They held the Constitution and the Holy Bible in contempt, and effectively rewrote the noble history of the United States in our public classrooms and institutions of "Higher Education." As Obama declared, "We are no longer a Christian nation!" I disagree! And so does President Trump!

Like President Reagan, who often declared, "America's best days are yet to come," I still believe there is hope. That is why I voted for Donald J. Trump to become President and supported his Movement to Make America Great Again. But I understand that that is not enough. You and I must now follow through and actively support the agenda to truly Make America Great Again!

I make known to my friends and associates and representatives in government that I support the Conservative agenda of President Trump, and I pray for America every day, and work to make the hope of that prayer a reality. As long as we have Americans of faith standing in the gap for this "last best hope for man on earth," there is hope that we can overcome this prolonged transformation of America by the Left.

We might be approaching the biblical cities of Sodom and Gomorrah, but we are not there yet. Not by a long shot, not on our watch, and definitely not as long as we still have young Americans standing watch on the walls of this bright shining city on a hill.

It's Morning Again in America! President Trump's State of the Union address on February 28, 2017, to a Joint Session of Congress and the American people made that perfectly clear! Let's make America great again!

It's Morning Again in America!

If my people, which are called by my name, shall humble themselves, and pray, and seek my face, and turn from their wicked ways; then will I hear from heaven, and will forgive their sin, and will heal their land.

~ 2 Chronicles 7:14

Chapter 3

The Silent Coup

Just found out that Obama had my 'wires tapped' in Trump Tower just before the victory.

How low has President Obama gone to tap my phones during the very sacred election process.

~ President Donald J. Trump
March 4, 2017

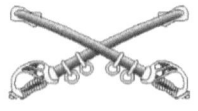

As I stated in the Introduction, there is in fact a silent coup underway in America. Some call it the work of a "Shadow Government" designed to undermine the Trump Administration. The coup is apparently led by none other than former President and "Community Organizer" Barack Hussein Obama, who is aided and abetted by a cast of characters. Those characters include: Democrats in Congress who are openly calling for the impeachment of President

Trump. Liberal insurgents in our federal judiciary who have substituted their will for the Law. And a well-entrenched Liberal Establishment in our intelligence apparatus, spurred on by the arguably unconstitutional acts of the previous Obama regime. All are bent on sabotaging the Trump agenda and finally pushing America into the ashbin of history's fallen superpowers. We cannot allow this to happen!

The Silent Coup I mentioned is not so silent any more, as even the Deputy Chair of the Democratic National Committee has called for the "Impeachment" of President Trump.[3] Other Democrat operatives have joined in the chorus as well. And if the Republican Party should lose its slim majority in the House of Representatives and the Senate in the 2018 midterm elections, that wishful thinking on the part of the Liberal Establishment to remove President Trump could become a reality. We cannot allow this to happen!

And of great concern to every American interested in preserving our constitutional rights is the charge by President Trump that his communications were tapped by the Obama regime. On the heels of what was bi-partisanly recognized as one of the greatest Presidential addresses to the Congress [on February 28, 2017] in American history, Liberal Establishment politicians led by Senate Minority Leader Chuck Schumer (Democrat – NY) unleashed a barrage of scurrilous charges against Attorney General Jeff Sessions, claiming he had perjured himself and secretly met with a Russian Ambassador. They recklessly call for Sec. Sessions' resignation. The slanderers in so doing attempted to draw attention away from the President's growing national support for his agenda to Make America Great Again. And the

---

[3] Minnesota Democrat & Muslim Rep. Keith Ellison, February 22, 2017.

saboteurs hinted other Trump Administration officials would soon enter their crosshairs.

In response, President Trump defended his cabinet and revealed the Silent Coup and its conspirators in a series of Saturday morning [March 4, 2017] Tweets directly to the American people:

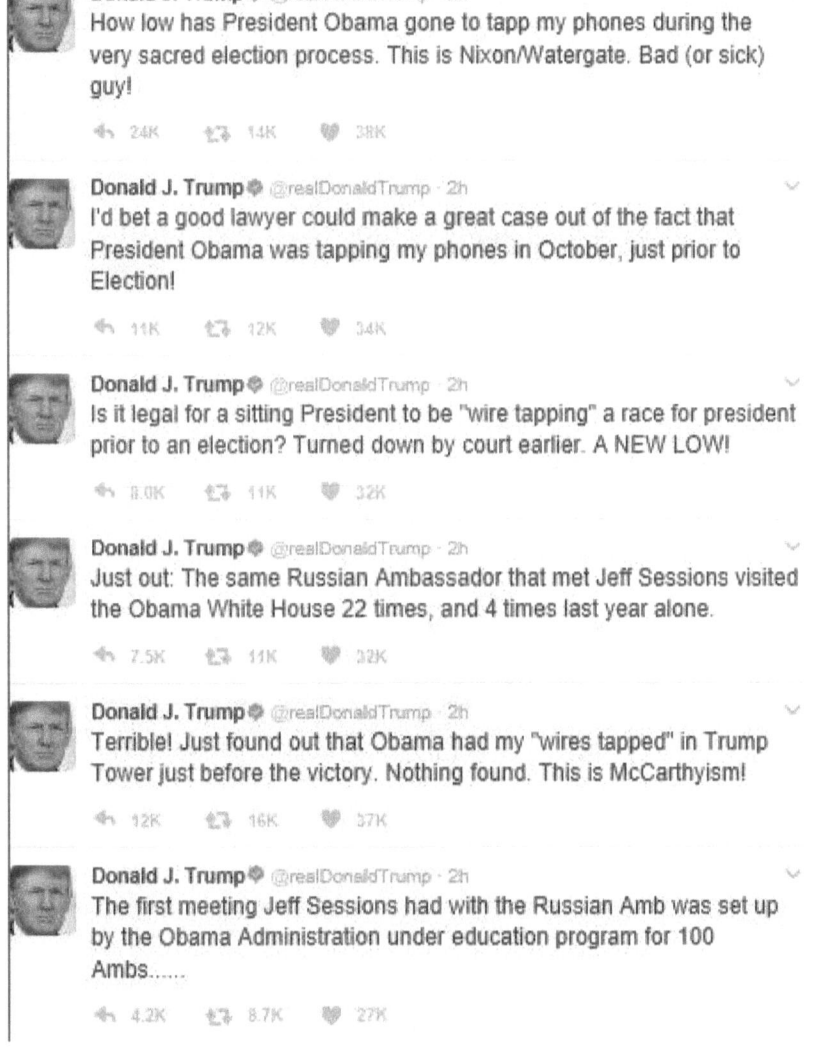

Donald J. Trump @realDonaldTrump · 2h
How low has President Obama gone to tapp my phones during the very sacred election process. This is Nixon/Watergate. Bad (or sick) guy!

24K   14K   38K

Donald J. Trump @realDonaldTrump · 2h
I'd bet a good lawyer could make a great case out of the fact that President Obama was tapping my phones in October, just prior to Election!

11K   12K   34K

Donald J. Trump @realDonaldTrump · 2h
Is it legal for a sitting President to be "wire tapping" a race for president prior to an election? Turned down by court earlier. A NEW LOW!

8.0K   11K   32K

Donald J. Trump @realDonaldTrump · 2h
Just out: The same Russian Ambassador that met Jeff Sessions visited the Obama White House 22 times, and 4 times last year alone.

7.5K   11K   32K

Donald J. Trump @realDonaldTrump · 2h
Terrible! Just found out that Obama had my "wires tapped" in Trump Tower just before the victory. Nothing found. This is McCarthyism!

12K   16K   37K

Donald J. Trump @realDonaldTrump · 2h
The first meeting Jeff Sessions had with the Russian Amb was set up by the Obama Administration under education program for 100 Ambs......

4.2K   8.7K   27K

Barack Hussein Obama was exposed! His attempted third-world-like coup to overthrow a constitutionally elected President was revealed to the light of day and an American public eager to hear the truth from our President on this social media platform. Americans have had enough of the Liberal Establishment filtering news through its fake news networks!

Multiple investigations into this alleged criminality by the former President and his accomplices are underway. Obama previously tapped the communications of reporter James Rosen of Fox News, along with his family, but now Obama was treading on the Constitution again, and this time with none other than the no-nonsense President of the United States elected to restore America's Rule of Law and respect for our constitutional republic. Obama, like most arrogant criminals, was reckless and crossed the line of acceptable behavior.

In truth, Probable Cause, that is, the reasonable likelihood a crime was committed, exists. And Law Enforcement can issue arrest warrants and indict Barack Hussein Obama and his co-conspirators for their high crimes and misdemeanors.

The bottom line is this: We are either a nation of laws, as I believe we are, or we are not, and those who died to defend the Rule of Law and our Constitution died in vain. It is time to test and fully embrace the legal maxim atop the Supreme Court, which states, "Equal Justice Under Law." In America, no one is above the Law!

These are perilous times. In my humble estimation, President Trump has a 2-year window of opportunity to substantially purge this Shadow Government, and arrest this Silent Coup. It is a cancer on the Constitution and our Founding Principles! We must root out, arrest, and deport the illegals currently registered to vote, with California being the largest culprit. President Trump must also deliver on his many campaign promises, not the least of which include deporting illegal criminals and building a great wall across our southern border with Mexico. He must use his "Bully Pulpit' to expose the slanderous obstructionists in Congress like Chuck Schumer and Nancy Pelosi for what they really are! Only then can we begin to undo the huge amount of damage caused by the Obama regime, and once again secure the blessings of liberty and freedom for this generation of Americans and the next! We can do it!

It's Morning Again in America!

But take heed, America:
Stand vigilant
and against this Silent Coup,
lest the republic be consumed by it ...

Cry "Havoc!" and let slip the dogs of war.

~ Mark Antony in Act 3, Scene 1, line 273
of William Shakespeare's *Julius Caesar*.
Mark Antony stands before the body of Julius Caesar
following his assassination, and exalts the Roman public to
take heed of the looming violence and breakdown of political
and civilized behavior as a direct result of the coup.

Chapter 4

The Barbarians at the Gates

In the first place we should insist that if the immigrant who comes here in good faith becomes an American and assimilates himself to us, he shall be treated on an exact equality with everyone else, for it is an outrage to discriminate against any man because of creed, or birthplace, or origin. But this is predicated upon the man's becoming in very fact an American.

~ President Theodore Roosevelt

Those who plot against our country will not be allowed to abuse our protections or our freedom.

~ Vice President Richard Cheney, November 15, 2001

Barack Hussein Obama did manage to keep one of his campaign promises of 2008: he fundamentally transformed America! Who would have believed that 16 years after the 9/11 attacks on America that we would now be a nation on the brink of welcoming tens of thousands Muslim so-called "refugees" into this shining city on a hill. These "refugees," predominantly military-age men, are surging through Europe and headed toward America. And these hordes have already left a path of destruction in their wake. The scene is reminiscent of the state of affairs that beset Rome some 1500 years ago.

Even more alarming, as I write these words, millions of illegal immigrants now roam the streets of America in violation of federal and state law. They have the blessing of law-breaking "Sanctuary State" governors and "Sanctuary City" mayors and councils, These illegals and their enablers are encouraged and emboldened in their lawlessness by the mainstream media and activist judges. They dwell amongst us and take advantage of legal safeguards and safety nets which were originally designed for legal citizens. This is a perversion of the Law. And these illegals are granted privileges that include free healthcare, welfare, immunity granted by their "sanctuary" hosts, and freedom to vote in any election without the benefit of having to prove who they are. While identification cards are required to receive access to the most basic resources in our society, illegal aliens, with the blessing of our courts, need not identify themselves through the production of an identification card in order to vote. The consequences of these foolish rulings are destructive to our culture. This invites the creation of an electorate and a system of government that is controlled by a plurality of noncitizens motivated to vote by their benefactors who prey on their desire to receive free benefits in return for keeping their enablers in office via the vote. It is a state of affairs our Founding Fathers warned us about in the early days of our republic. It is self-destructive!

Americans soundly rejected the establishment politicians who reside in all three branches of government, and here I most certainly include the judiciary. It is why we have Donald J. Trump serving as President!

But there is much work to do! The past eight years were particularly harmful to America's foundation. 2015, in particular, marked a turning point for the judiciary in America. For the first time in our history as a Republic, the Supreme Court of the United States violated the Constitution in a number of rulings. In its June *King v. Burwell* decision, six of the nine justices on the Supreme Court substituted their will for the will of the Congress, and enabled the implementation of ObamaCare to proceed. These justices became lawmakers by substituting the words of Congress in its statutory law for their own words. This was done in violation of their duty under the Constitution and to the people of the United States of America. They violated a sacred trust!

In *Obergefell v. Hodges*, the Supreme Court rewrote more than 5000 years of established law with regard to marital relations, and gave a new definition to marriage. They did this by manufacturing a connection between the homosexual lifestyle and the protections afforded American citizens under the Constitution. A razor-thin majority on the Court substituted their will for the Law and usurped the Constitution, in a manner much like they did to justify the murder of millions of unborn American citizens through abortion. In *Rowe v. Wade*, the Court expanded the notion of "privacy" to such an extent as to allow mothers to be exploited by abortionists and baby parts sellers to actually kill their babies. And the Court did this without regard to the constitutional protections of the babies under the Fifth Amendment to the Constitution, which states, "No person shall be...deprived of life, liberty, or property, without due process of law."

These millions of aborted babies since the high Court's decision were most certainly deprived of life and liberty. It is a national disgrace and a level of barbarism rivalling Nazi Germany. This is the evidence that America has ceased to be great.

It is my hope in the years to come that America investigates and conducts a Nuremburg-like prosecution of these butchers who killed these babies and profited from the sale of their body parts. There is no statute of limitations on murder, and if murder and other violations of law were committed, they should and must be prosecuted. The excuse of "I was only following orders" or "It was acceptable under [Nazi] law to do so" will not be an adequate defense.

Literally minutes after the *Obergefell* decision, I was on Christian Radio WECC The Lighthouse with its president, Paul Hafer, sharing my views on the unprecedented move by the Supreme Court to redefine marriage, which is specifically in the jurisdiction of the states, and aid Obama in the radical transformation of America and Western Civilization. The Constitution was being dismantled before our very eyes. The high Court was aiding the Executive Branch in usurping the Constitution, and the Republican-led Congress was disavowing its sworn duty and multiple promises to the American people to stop it.

For the first time in my life, as I drove home from the court on that fateful Friday in June 2015, I seriously wondered, what good is a Supreme Court that forsakes its duty under the Constitution to support the tyrannical agenda of a chief executive, in this case, Barack Hussein Obama?

The unprecedented rise of outsiders to the political process we witnessed in the 2016 Presidential race is evidence of the broad-based rejection by the American people of politics as usual. And fuelling that rejection was the conduct of so-called "opposition-party" leaders in the GOP like Senate Majority Leader Mitch McConnell and former House Speaker John Boehner and Paul Ryan. These men were given a mandate and control of the American Congress to oppose the fundamentally flawed transformational agenda of Barack Hussein Obama. They utterly failed, and in many instances, enabled that destructive agenda to succeed. It was a betrayal of the sacred trust bestowed upon these men by the American people.

On issue after issue, be it ObamaCare or the treaty masquerading as an executive deal by Obama, the Republican leadership in Congress failed the American people.

A consequence of Barack Hussein Obama's fundamental transformation of America includes the death of the great American Spirit. This can be seen in a mindset that doubts America's exceptionalism. This is manifest in a multitude of naysayers who believe the construction of a great wall along the border with Mexico, the deportation of millions of illegal criminals, and the repeal and replacement of Obama care with an affordable and exceptional healthcare system is impossible. And this is said in a country that has been endowed by God with the ability to do the impossible. We survived and prospered after a horrific civil war that pit brother against brother, went on to win two world wars, cured many of the so-called incurable diseases, and landed a man on the moon and returned him safely to the earth.

With all the exceptional things America has accomplished, like building the Panama Canal through the Western Hemisphere, providing emergency relief and medicine to the world, and being a beacon of hope, just to name a few, I am stunned by the doubters. We actually have citizens, and men and women aspiring to the highest office in the land, saying America can no longer do great things! How very sad.

They say, "Deporting twelve million illegals is impossible!" They claim, "Building a great wall on our southern border is [also] impossible!" They just don't know America!

That is one of the reasons I gravitated to the candidacy and Movement of Donald J. Trump. He was – and remains -- a steadfast visionary with bold, exceptional ideas, and the grit and resolve to make them happen! America needs such leaders once again, and thank God we have one such leader in President Trump!

Not since Ronald Reagan have we had such a President! And not since Ronald Reagan have we had a President more opposed by the establishment wing of their party than President Trump! Yet, this is happening on a smaller level in Senate and congressional House races across the country, and I know about it firsthand. I felt the same contempt for new solutions and ideas when I ran for Maryland's 5th Congressional District seat in the U.S. House of Representatives as an outsider in 1994.

And as the bell tolls, calling us to close yet another chapter in the history of the United States, we look back. Sometimes with mixed emotions, we recall the past century as a time of great change, unprecedented growth, and unparalleled triumphs and tragedies. Through it all, America has withstood the test of time. America still represents what President Reagan called that "bright shining city on a hill," and what he and President Lincoln foretold was "the last best hope for man on earth."

Today, as the Islamist State spreads like a plague across the globe, America flounders with $20 trillion dollars of debt, with a Congress and a Judiciary seemingly dead set on obstructing the President in discharging his sacred duty to protect America!

We must recognize and meet the enemy within. But this will not happen with a Congress that has been complicit in America's demise. And much like the great Roman Empire, just before the dawn of the Dark Ages, America has embarked well down that perilous path of moral decline, a dismantling of her military establishment, and compromise with the barbarians at the gate. The terrorists who perpetrated the September 11th atrocities were barbarians. In fact, they were all Muslims. They travelled from the Middle East, most from Saudi Arabia to be exact, and most entered this country legally, through a liberal American immigration policy. That same immigration policy allows students from terrorist and terrorist-sponsoring nations to enter this country on student visas, benefit from our superior educational system, engage in activities that their countries of origin would never allow on their own soil, and return to their countries to ultimately work against the national interests of America. It is a counterproductive policy, and ultimately self-defeating. Those who perpetrated the heinous acts of terrorism against innocent Americans violated the spirit and letter of the law that allows foreigners the privilege to visit our shores.

The horrendous and unrelenting terrorist attacks by the jihadists serve as a somber and prophetic warning about the true nature and objective of Islam. It foretells what we can expect if we accept these Muslim "refugees" into America. Islam is a culture obsessed with the destruction of Western Civilization. They are bent on returning the world to the Dark

Ages. They possess neither the desire nor inclination to coexist with anything other than their fanatical brethren. This is what the Koran teaches. The sooner we realize this, the safer and better we will be.

To its credit, France has declared it will close down mosques that preach hate. America should do the same! And President Trump, to his credit, is the only official who is open to the same course of action. Mosques operating as classrooms for these jihadist terrorists that masquerade as places of worship should be closed, and their "teachers" imprisoned or deported.

The shear history of Islam's barbarism should have resulted in a heightened state of security within America's borders, but Obama and his allies in Congress were actually dropping America's defences and inviting in the very barbarians who aim to destroy our culture. The treachery of these politicians foreshadows an ominous future, unless we act with firm resolve to support President Trump and remove those members of Congress from office, replace them with statesmen who recognize the threat, and act to make America great again!

George Washington once wrote to John Adams on the subject of American citizenship. Washington's vision was to have immigrants "assimilated to our customs, measures and laws." It was the hope of Washington that native-born citizens and immigrants, shortly after their arrival in America, would "soon become one people."

On the very birth of this nation as a bonafide World Power (following the Spanish-American War), President Theodore Roosevelt declared, "In the first place we should insist that if the immigrant who comes here in good faith becomes an American and assimilates himself to us, he shall be treated on an exact equality with everyone else, for it is an outrage to discriminate against any man because of creed, or birthplace, or origin. But this is predicated upon the man's becoming in very fact an American."

We cannot allow barbarians to enter this nation, nor can we afford to treat them like U.N. diplomats in these Democrat-created "sanctuary cities" and allow them to violate our laws—all in the hope they will "assimilate" and become civilized, as if by some magic. These barbarians now behead, crucify, and drown Christians in cages in the Middle East. They are fulfilling the dictates of their "holy book," and living the purest form of Islam. These barbarians can never become Americans! To think otherwise is folly.

Washington and Roosevelt were well aware of the consequences of a divided nation, when barbarians are brought into the fold, and we exist as a country divided. President Trump knows this as well. Inherent in being an American, and understanding and assimilating our customs, traditions and laws, is the English language. There is nothing wrong with a knowledge of foreign languages, but there is a problem when we have bilingual education, and multilingual applications for driver's licenses, welfare, and voter registration, just to name a few.

I can just envision a future presidential election being disputed because the government failed to include all known languages on all ballots. Maybe I am giving some future political partisan an idea to contest another presidential election in the future. Bad enough in 2000 the Democrats complained in Florida that the "butterfly" ballot, which was introduced and approved by the Democrats, somehow discriminated against people who voted for Gore. Apparently they couldn't muster the intelligence to follow an arrow to a candidate's name and make a choice. America is better than that! We were founded as an English-speaking, God-fearing nation of immigrants.

The last time I looked, our Declaration of Independence and Constitution were written in English. Our laws, state and federal, are written in English. Our currency is replete with words written in English, including the phrase, "In God We Trust." And English is the common language that binds the many in this Nation as one people. A country of many "official" languages is a divided and weak country. The growing politically correct practice of "language inclusiveness," evidenced by the plethora of languages we see on government publications in urban areas, greatly contribute to the dividing and weakening of our nation. The Roman Empire, in its final days, gave testimony to that.

The integrity of America's territorial borders is another serious matter. If we are serious about stopping the flow of illegal immigrants, we must also be serious about stopping illegal immigration through our southern border, along with the illegal contraband they carry, not the least of which is drugs.

This is why I support the bold ideas of President Trump, including the building of a great wall along our border with Mexico, and having the Mexican government pay for it. This is most certainly not an "impossible" or "cost-prohibitive" feat! And the ancillary benefits to such an undertaking would be excellent American jobs in construction, maintenance, transportation, security, and tourism. It is a win-win proposition for America!

We must also seriously contemplate deploying American military forces along our border with Mexico until that wall is built. The Border Patrol, as good as it is, lacks sufficient resources to get the job done! Among other things, we must seriously contemplate a re-evaluation of America's longstanding immigration policies, particularly when it comes to the issuance of student visas to so-called "students" from known-terrorist and terrorist-sponsoring states. We must stop this practice of issuing student visas to immigrants from terrorist and terrorist-sponsoring nations immediately! If Congress is serious about combating terrorists and those who harbor them, we must remove these individuals from our homeland, especially those who use a legal status to perpetrate illegal acts. We admit foreigners from terrorist and terrorist-sponsoring nations into America through a liberal immigration scheme, and we wonder why the enemy walks amongst us.

We must overhaul the immigration policies that have brought us to this point of peril. And we must have the resolve to do so immediately. It will take a considerable amount of time and resources for the United States to adequately safeguard her borders, but it must be done. The worldwide terrorist threats against America demand nothing less, especially if we are to survive and prosper, and fulfill our role as the world's last best hope for freedom.

America is still that shining city on a hill President Reagan spoke about and the Bible foretold. We have prospered like no other country. We have served as the hope of a dark and dangerous world. We are Americans! It's Morning Again in America!

The terrorist enemy that threatens civilization today is unlike any we have ever known. It slaughters thousands of innocents-a crime of war and a crime against humanity. It seeks weapons of mass destruction and threatens their use against America. No one should doubt the intent, nor the depth, of its consuming, destructive hatred. Terrorist operatives infiltrate our communities – plotting, planning and waiting to kill again. They enjoy the benefits of our free society even as they commit themselves to our destruction. They exploit our openness-not randomly or haphazardly-but by deliberate, premeditated design.

~ Attorney General John Ashcroft, December 6, 2001

Chapter 5

A New Call to Crusade

We will reinforce old alliances and form new ones – and unite the civilized world against Radical Islamic Terrorism, which we will eradicate completely from the face of the Earth.

~ President Donald J. Trump, January 20, 2017

It seems that a New Knighthood has recently appeared on the earth...a new kind of knighthood and one unknown to the ages gone by. It ceaselessly wages a twofold war both against flesh and blood and against a spiritual army of evil in the heavens...He is truly a fearless knight and secure on every side, for his soul is protected by the armour of faith just as his body is protected by armour of steel. He is thus doubly armed and need fear neither demons nor men.

~ Cistercian abbot Bernard of Clairvaux,
on behalf of the Knights Templar,
a religious military order born out of the First Crusade,
12th Century, A.D.

I often consider the words of President Reagan in the final days of his administration, when he said, "America's best days are yet to come!" There have been times I have doubted his prophecy, and hope has waned. But I have come to understand that to truly be an American one must undergo the fatigues of supporting the American dream of our Founding Fathers. And more importantly, I have come to understand that one is never without hope if we are at peace with who we are and where our power comes from. America has prospered so much, and has become a shining city on a hill, because of the faith we have in our Creator and His hand upon us as a Christian nation.

If you were to read the following in any newspaper today, you might rightly conclude the author was speaking about the rampaging Muslim State and its ISIS soldiers:

"...a race from the kingdom of the Persians...has invaded the lands of those Christians and has depopulated them by the sword, pillage and fire; it has led away a part of the captives into its own country, and a part it has destroyed by cruel tortures; it has either entirely destroyed the churches of God or appropriated them for the rites of its own religion. They destroy the altars, after having defiled them with their uncleanness."

However, they are the words of Pope Urban II, and they were uttered just over 920 years ago! But the events that led to this declaration go back even further into antiquity.

The Great Roman Empire breathed its last breath on September 4, 476 AD, when the last Roman Emperor, Romulus Augustus, was deposed by the barbarians. But this event was preceded by a number of significant national disasters, such as the sacking of what Saint Augustine called "The City of God" in 410 AD by the Visigoths, and again by the Vandals in 455 AD. And although historians may debate the events that brought about the end of Pax Romana, there is no debate that the death of Rome brought about the Dark Ages, a time when infidels stripped the earth of those treasures which enlighten men and gave them hope. It was truly a time when a dark shroud descended upon the face of the earth, a season of desolation.

But Almighty God, in His infinite wisdom, preserved a magnificent remnant, a few points of light in an otherwise lost and desolate world. These were the Crusaders who set out on a Quest to protect Christian pilgrims from slaughter at the hands of Muslims in the Holy Lands. They personified the Armor of God in lands that were shrouded in the darkness of Islam. These were lands that held unspeakable horrors to anyone that would not convert to their culture. Beheadings, crucifixions, and other forms of murder were their common practice to people outside of their perverse "faith." They had a particular dislike of Christians, and relished in the destruction of any symbols of Christendom. They were, in the words of Pope Urban II, "an accursed race, a race utterly alienated from

God." Little has changed in the last millennium.

This was the mission and essence of the First Crusade, a commitment to a noble cause to protect the rights of Christians wherever they may be, rooted in a firm belief that God had a purpose for those who feared Him and lived according to His Word. And of these brave men who took part in this Crusade, this was said by Cistercian abbot Bernard of Clairvaux:

"It appears that a New Knighthood has recently appeared on the earth...a new kind of knighthood and one unknown to the ages gone by. It ceaselessly wages a twofold war against flesh and blood and against a spiritual army of evil in the heavens...He is truly a fearless knight and secure on every side, for his soul is protected by the armor of faith just as his body is protected by armor of steel. He is thus doubly armed and need fear neither demons nor men." And so it was!

The Crusader was a man of God, and the achievement of the First Crusade was a miracle! It was the major step of mankind out of the Dark Ages, a time when the light of Rome was extinguished and a mere remnant of Christianity flickered like a lone candle light amidst a dark and desolate world. It stemmed the tide of barbarians who sought to oppress the world, and eradicate the illuminating literary works of man that gave hope and enlightenment to all mankind.

And this First Crusade was sparked by Pope Urban II at the Council of Clermont in 1095. It was here the Roman Catholic pontiff addressed a great multitude, and spoke as a prophet.

The Pope urged all Christians to go to the aid of fellow-Christians under attack by the Muslims and to recover the Holy Land from their tyrannical rule. These are his words, as remembered and recorded by the men who were present and heard him:

> From the confines of Jerusalem and the city of Constantinople a horrible tale has gone forth and very frequently has been brought to our ears, namely, that a race from the kingdom of the Persians, an accursed race, a race utterly alienated from God, a generation forsooth which has not directed its heart and has not entrusted its spirit to God, has invaded the lands of those Christians and has depopulated them by the sword, pillage and fire; it has led away a part of the captives into its own country, and a part it has destroyed by cruel tortures; it has either entirely destroyed the churches of God or appropriated them for the rites of its own religion. They destroy the altars, after having defiled them with their uncleanness. They circumcise the Christians, and the blood of the circumcision they either spread upon the altars or pour into the vases of the baptismal font.

> When they wish to torture people by a base death, they perforate their navels, and dragging forth the extremity of the intestines, bind it to a stake; then with flogging they lead the victim around until the viscera having gushed forth the victim falls prostrate upon the ground. Others they bind to a post and pierce with arrows. Others they compel to extend their necks and

then, attacking them with naked swords, attempt to cut through the neck with a single blow. What shall I say of the abominable rape of the women? To speak of it is worse than to be silent.

Moreover, you who are to go shall have us praying for you; we shall have you fighting for God's people. It is our duty to pray, yours to fight against the Amalekites. With Moses, we shall extend unwearied hands in prayer to Heaven, while you go forth and brandish the sword, like dauntless warriors, against Amalek.[4]

In the Old Testament, specifically 1 Samuel 15:1-7, we read about the Amalekites the Pope referenced. It was here, through the prophet Samuel, that God charged King Saul with a great quest:

[1]Samuel also said unto Saul, The LORD sent me to anoint thee to be king over his people, over Israel: now therefore hearken thou unto the voice of the words of the LORD.
[2] Thus saith the LORD of hosts, I remember that which Amalek did to Israel, how he laid wait for him in the way, when he came up from Egypt.
[3] **Now go and smite Amalek, and utterly destroy all that they have, and spare them not; but slay both man and woman, infant and suckling, ox and sheep, camel and ass.**

---

[4] Krey, A.C. (1921). *The First Crusade: The Accounts of Eyewitnesses and Participants.* Princeton, 33-36.

⁴ And Saul gathered the people together, and numbered them in Telaim, two hundred thousand footmen, and ten thousand men of Judah.

⁵ And Saul came to a city of Amalek, and laid wait in the valley.

⁶ And Saul said unto the Kenites, Go, depart, get you down from among the Amalekites, lest I destroy you with them: for ye shewed kindness to all the children of Israel, when they came up out of Egypt. So the Kenites departed from among the Amalekites.

⁷ And Saul smote the Amalekites from Havilah until thou comest to Shur, that is over against Egypt.

However, Saul disobeyed the voice of God and spared the King of Amalek and many of his possessions.[5] This ultimately cost Saul his reign, his life, and the life of his sons and a great many other Israelites.[6] This same mistake would not be made by the First Crusaders.

This was the calling of the First Crusade, to demonstrate the power of Almighty God in those who love Him and are called according to His purpose.[7] They followed the Great Commission: "Go ye into all the world, and preach the gospel to every creature."[8] They did this, and defended the faithful and the weak. They were more than conquerors, they liberated civilization from the death-grip of Islam.

---

[5] 1 Samuel 15:8-28.
[6] 1 Samuel 31:1-7.
[7] Romans 8:28.
[8] Mark 16:15.

This was a Quest issued by the Pope, and it gave birth to a new morning in the Holy Land and the Kingdom of Jerusalem on July 15, 1099, when a victorious Christian army raised the Cross of Christ once again in the City of David. This culminating event ushered in the end of the Dark Ages, and the founding of a bright shining city on a hill. Pax Britannia and the current Pax Americana are proof of this positive transformation.

Such a calling is needed today, not only to stem the rising tide of Islamic terror in the world, but to unite the West against this common enemy. Islam itself claims to be incompatible with Western Civilization, and has demonstrated its true nature in the rise of the Islamic State in the Middle East. Instituting Sharia Law, these barbarians have systematically exterminated Christians in their conquered territories through beheadings, crucifixions, stonings and a host of other atrocities. Virtually nothing has changed in the barbarous practices of this degenerate culture since the time of Pope Urban II. Such are the ways of Islam when they gain control. To speak such of Islam is not Islamophopic, it is Truth!

The Muslims in Iran have already called for "Death to America," and have pledged to "Wipe Israel off the face of the map!" I take them at their word. Islam is an existential threat to Western Civilization.

America and the West would do well to stop the migration of this alien culture, and demand their adherence to the minimum rules of civility wherever they may be. To do less would be an invitation to another Dark Age on the planet. And to do nothing would mean the annihilation of countless Christians and Jews across the globe.

Islam can be stopped, but it will take a coalition of the willing, led by the only power on earth with the resources, resolve, and moral authority to take up the Crusade and succeed. This Crusade, against the Islamic State and their worldwide caliphate, has the potential of uniting Western Civilization against a common enemy more than any other in a millennium. Even the Russians and the Chinese could be found as allies in this great cause. The Russians as I write are pounding ISIS and their fellow-Muslims in Syria. In the words of Pope Urban II, "Let therefore hatred depart from among you, let your quarrels end, let wars cease, and let all dissensions and controversies slumber. Enter upon the road to the Holy Sepulchre; wrest that land from the wicked race, and subject it to yourselves."

The Crusades were a great force for Good! They blunted Islam's aggression and ended the Dark Ages a millennium ago ... and they can be reconstituted again for that purpose!

It's Morning Again in America

Today, our nation saw evil. None of us will ever forget this day, yet we go forward to defend freedom and all that is good and just in our world. Terrorist attacks can shake the foundations of our biggest buildings, but they cannot touch the foundation of America. These acts shatter steel, but they cannot dent the steel of American resolve. Those who make war against the United States have chosen their own destruction.

~ President George W. Bush

In a time when evil and darkness seems to prevail, Christ tells us once again, "Fear not!"

~ Pope John Paul II

Chapter 6

God and Country

God presides over the destinies of nations.

~ Patrick Henry

It is the duty of all Nations to acknowledge the providence of Almighty God.

~ President George Washington,
First Presidential Proclamation, October 3, 1789

America was founded by people who believe[d] that God was their rock of safety. I recognize we must be cautious in claiming that God is on our side, but I think it's all right to keep asking if we're on His side. The time has come to turn to God and reassert our trust in Him for the healing of America...Our country is in need of and ready for a spiritual renewal.

~ President Ronald Reagan

It is hard to argue that the protective hand of God has not been on America. From our very birth as a nation, we have done what no other people ever did in the history of man. We were the first to gain independence from the Crown on the simple proposition that men are "endowed by their Creator with certain unalienable Rights, that among these are Life, Liberty and the pursuit of Happiness—That to secure these rights, governments are instituted among men, deriving their just power from the consent of the governed." It was indeed revolutionary, and we succeeded!

We have since led the world in justice, technology, scientific discovery, humanitarian outreach, tolerance of religion—you name the noble cause, and America has been there! One of the undeniable truths in this country is the faith of our Founding Fathers. They were men of God, who acted upon their beliefs. The fact we are a nation built upon a Christian heritage is undeniable! This fact is evident in the Declaration of Independence, the Constitution, and virtually every document of American historical substance. Seals on licenses, commissions and other official documents refer to "the year of our Lord." Even our money bears the motto, "In God We Trust." Our state and national legislatures and courts all refer to God at one time or another during session. Our Congress begins each day with an opening prayer. Examples abound!

Nevertheless, our Christian heritage and traditions are under attack. We are bombarded by attacks from the left to quash any reference to God in our daily lives. But for what purpose, and to what end? Throughout our country, we have attacks on displays of the Ten Commandments and prayer in public places (not Islamic chanting, mind you), and classes that teach good citizenship. But the battlefront does not end there. Even reference to the Ten Commandments is under assault in our nation's courtrooms. Imagine that! Simple nativity scenes in our local communities during Christmas time are openly, and many times successfully, challenged in courtrooms across the land. And the list goes on and on. What is amazing, however, is not the fact people object to any reference of God. The amazing thing is that we have people in responsible positions willing to entertain and support such agendas, and, unfortunately, many of them are sitting legislators and federal judges. Think about it!

Just this past year, the Supreme Court of the United States has taken it upon itself to redefine marriage to accommodate a vocal minority that sought not so much to achieve "equal rights under the law," as they stated, but to destroy an institution (Marriage) that was defined by God and embraced by civilizations for thousands of years.

During what has been called the Greatest Generation, that is, the World War II generation of my father, the thought of American lawyers, Congressman and Senators rallying to the aid of terrorists being treated humanely in the Caribbean while American soldiers were fighting and dying abroad would have been unthinkable! But, alas, this is a new day! We not only have Senators looking out for the so-called "rights" of the Taliban and al-Qaida terrorists at Guantanamo Bay in Cuba, we have Obama and Hillary Clinton rallying to the cause of the Muslim terrorists. Incredible! They give aid and comfort to the enemy.

Islam in its purest form proclaims itself incompatible with Western Civilization. Why are we disputing it? Better yet, why are our established political leaders in Washington denying it?

I realize such statements are controversial. Throughout my many years as both a student and a teacher I have heard the old adage of never mix religion with politics. I have come to discover the complete lack of wisdom in that proposition. Politics is a struggle between ideas. What greater struggle exists in our day and age than that which can be found in the war of religious ideas. For Christians, that struggle is found in the spiritual realm. We followed the dictates of Holy Scripture, the foremost of which is the teaching of Jesus Christ. It is a religion of peace and good will.

Islam, on the other hand, is a political movement masquerading as a religion. It is a fanatical movement steeped in violence, intolerance, and the eradication of the infidel. Unfortunately for Christians, we are the infidels, along with our Jewish brethren. It is not a movement of coexistence. And it is an existential threat to the American way of life, the West, and all of Christendom. This is not my opinion, it is an historical fact. And we can ignore it at our own peril, or in the words of Shakespeare, we can take arms against the struggle and by opposing, end it! This was the central meaning of the Crusades. They were a great force for good that confronted evil in their time, defeated it, and ended what was known as the Muslim Dark Ages.

We as a nation and as a people of Western Civilization would do well to remember the lessons of the Crusades. When evil is confronted, it is stopped. When good men do nothing in the face of evil, it triumphs.

As I write this work, President Donald J Trump is keeping his campaign promises to the people of America. He outlined and now pursues a number of initiatives to make America great again: build a great wall, deport illegal criminals and the jihadist "refugees" Obama welcomed to America, end ObamaCare, stop the persecution of Christians, and recognize that the government is a servant of the people, and not their ruler.

However, President Trump needs our help! His message is under fire by the Democrat Party, its allies in the Judiciary, and their propaganda arm in the mainstream media. But the more President Trump speaks of these issues, the more popular he becomes, and the greater the threat he poses to the establishment that prefers the status quo it had under Obama. President Trump is the target of their personal attacks. Their thinking is: if you can kill the messenger, you kill the message!

So the question becomes: which is more important, the messenger or the message? In this case, each is dependent on the other. President Trump is the messenger and the leader of the Movement to Make America Great Again. For the Movement to succeed, President Trump must succeed! So I say, if the liberal politicians and the status quo establishment succeed in defeating President Trump, they will also succeed in defeating his initiatives he champions to make America great again. We cannot allow this to happen!

Because of President Trump's success thus far, liberal talking points and fake news narratives have dominated the conversation, especially in the mass media and social platforms. This is the propaganda of the Left, and tactics I personally witnessed employed against President Ronald Reagan.

In today's world, we have every right to be skeptical, especially when we look at the current leadership of our Republican Congress. These were men who were given majorities to stop Obama's agenda, and not only failed to stop it but wound up enabling it. Some question President Trump's sincerity as a populist conservative. I do not! And I believe people can learn and grow and change their minds on certain issues. That's a part of life. But I do abhor politicians who make promises knowing full well they never meant to keep them. These are the leaders we see in the modern GOP. Politicians like John McCain and Lindsey Graham. These politicians are rightfully called "RINOs" (Republicans in Name Only). I do not put President Trump in this category. He has pledged to devote the full measure of his life to preserving this last best hope for man on earth. I believe him! I support him!

Now is the time to elect Conservative-Republican representatives at the local and national level who will champion a return to traditional family values and common sense! The alternative is a further erosion of the foundations upon which our country was built. And that alternative is simply unacceptable! Why not base our fundamental core curriculum in grade schools back to the 3 Rs and the C, that is, Reading, [W]riting, [A]rithmatic, and [Good] Citizenship? And then reinforce those concepts throughout life? They served us well during the Greatest Generation and years before. Are we now too sophisticated, too technologically advanced a people to build a bridge of honor and integrity back to our Founding Principles and the fundamental values that made us a superpower and the moral example to the world in the 20th Century? I pray not!

We have much to learn from the honor and traditions of the past, and those legions of American patriots that came before us. And history is replete with the downfall of nations who thought themselves infinitely wiser than their predecessors and Almighty God. The Tower of Babel and Sodom and Gomorrah immediately come to mind. God and country — I have dedicated my life to both.

During my own time as a youth, I recall a simple recitation we had in grade school following the morning prayer. It was written about America in 1740, and set to music in February of 1832 by Samuel F. Smith. It has always served me well, and gave me pause to reflect on the past and my duty in the present. And it went exactly like this:

My country 'tis of thee, Sweet land of liberty, Of thee I sing; Land where my fathers died, Land of the pilgrim's pride, From every mountain side, Let freedom ring... Our fathers' God to thee, Author of liberty, To thee we sing. Long may our land be bright, With freedom's holy light, Protect us by they might, Great God, our King.

So, in this day and age, when good is called evil and evil good, and when men who embrace our Founding Principles and quest to make America great again are called "racist" or "homophobic" or "islamophobic," let us chart a new course, one that embraces our love of God and country. I am old enough to recall the same epitaphs being hurled at Ronald Reagan in 1980, when he chose as an outsider to stand against the establishment to make America great again! But this is a new day in America, one of opportunity and genuine hope under President Trump. Let us embrace it!

It's Morning Again in America!

Americans are not a perfect people, but we are called to a perfect mission.

I thank God that my life has been spent in a land of liberty, and that he has given me a heart to love my country with the affection of a son.

~ President Andrew Jackson

Chapter 7

Our Rendezvous with Destiny

You and I have a rendezvous with destiny. We will preserve for our children this, the last best hope of man on earth, or we will sentence them to take the first step into a thousand years of darkness.

If we fail, at least let our children and our children's children say of us we justified our brief moment here. We did all that could be done.

~ President Ronald Reagan

President Ronald Reagan was a Great Communicator, but first and foremost he was a Great American. He was a man of faith, with a vision for our country, gifted with the ability to powerfully communicate his ideas. His patriotism resonated throughout our country. And it was his genuine love of America that fueled his resolve to bring our country back from the brink. Quite simply, he inspired the best in us!

On more than one occasion, President Reagan declared, "I believe that God put this land between two great oceans to be found by a special people from every corner of the world who had that extra love of freedom that prompted them to leave their homeland and come to this land to make it a brilliant light beam of freedom to the world."

President Reagan understood and communicated America's exceptionalism. His was the genius of a simple message: "Let's Make America Great Again!" And he applied this biblical admonishment to himself and this blessed land: "For unto whomsoever much is given, of him shall be much required: and to whom men have committed much, of him they will ask the more."[9] His leadership and faith made me a believer and crusader in the cause.

President Reagan unashamedly called America "a Christian nation" that "was blessed by God," and generously shared his faith in God. This was the strength and success of the Reagan Revolution!

With that said, I first met Governor Ronald Reagan in 1980. He was on the campaign trail with Congressman Jack Kemp in Queens, New York. He was seeking the presidency, and I was a graduate student at St. John's University. Governor

---

[9] Luke 12:48.

Reagan was my hero, because he loved America and worked tirelessly to improve her, and he embodied the ideals that made America great. But when I first met him, and shook his hand, America was in decline. The liberal politicians lost the War in Vietnam, Jimmy Carter was our impotent president, and the torch of liberty had not so dimmed in our two-hundred-plus years of history. We were on a precipice. As candidate Ronald Reagan said on that fateful day,

"You and I have a rendezvous with destiny.
We will preserve for our children this,
the last best hope of man on earth,
or we will sentence them to take the first step
into a thousand years of darkness.
If we fail, at least let our children and our children's children
say of us we justified our brief moment here.
We did all that could be done."

It was a pivotal moment in the history of our republic. And later that year, Ronald Reagan was elected the 40th President of the United States, and America began her march down the long road to recovery. His campaign slogan was "Let's Make America Great Again!" I accepted it as his pledge to lead a national crusade to bring America back from the brink. Praise God, President Reagan kept that pledge!

President Ronald Reagan was the right man, at the right time, to lead America back to greatness! And this book is a tribute to this great, good man, as much as it is a tribute to the enduring American Spirit!

I continue to herald the virtues of President Reagan, even to the present day. He was a great leader and visionary! And he taught us much about America, and the leadership it needs to survive and prosper. He brought America back, and in the process changed many lives, including mine. He became president less than a month before his 70th birthday, and changed my perspective on age. President Reagan was a favorite and champion of both the young and old. So much so, he was often mocked and trivialized by the liberal media pundits, but he soundly defeated Jimmy Carter and changed the political landscape of the South. And that same liberal media questioned his conservative agenda for America, but he managed to win re-election by a landslide, achieving victory in 49 of the 50 states in our Union, and coming very close to winning the home state of his democrat opponent. President Reagan gave no quarter to his opponents, defeating them in their liberal strongholds. He surrendered no states in the electoral process. All were contested and in play. He made an end to abortion, reduced taxes, and national defense Republican issues. He rebuilt our military and restored the great American Spirit.

We often hear fellow-Americans, including myself, say, "We need another President Reagan." The country longs for a return to true leaders, who openly and honestly champion the values of America, a God-blessed Citadel and a "shining city on a hill." I believe we now have such a leader in the Oval Office!

As I write this words, I believe we do have in our midst a select group of bold Americans with a firm belief in America's

Exceptionalism. And first among these is President Donald J. Trump. Not since President Ronald Reagan has the Republican Party been so poised to reconstitute the Great American Spirit as we are with President Trump!

Back in 1988, I was an Army officer assigned to an outpost in a hostile land. No, it wasn't some foreign battlefield, it was an American college campus, the University of Massachusetts to be exact. I was assigned there as an R.O.T.C. instructor. It was one of those tours of duty Army officers dread, because it takes you out of the field and away from your troops, and places you in an unfriendly environment of civilians who are often vocal about their contempt for traditional American values and the military. The worst of the bunch were the tenured professors who entered academia long before to escape military service to pursue their utopian philosophies of world peace under the very blanket of protection provided by the police and military they held in contempt. You see that on many college campuses today … but in that respect, the University of Massachusetts led the way!

It was during that time I first wrote to then-businessman and entrepreneur Donald J. Trump of New York. It was a letter I wrote with questions on a book he had just written and I had just read, *The Art of the Deal*. I asked Mr. Trump a series of questions on dealing with difficult civilian leaders and influencing them to modify their belief systems.

I was not surprised to receive a response, and it was a handwritten reply from Donald J. Trump himself. It was a cornucopia of leadership and management observations and instructions, and they made a lasting impression on me. In fact, I have applied the principles since, and they have always served me well!

I came to find out in later years that Trump was also a student of President Reagan, and an admirer of him as well, although it may not have always appeared so to the casual observer. President Reagan was, as Trump would confess on the campaign trail in 2015, next to his father and mother, a major example of a life well-lived, and someone to emulate.

President Reagan was, and continues to be, a shining example of what public service and political leadership are all about: Duty, Honor, Country. His life's work for America is something worth remembering and honoring, and we can do that by being the voices through which new generations of Americans re-discover the wonderful and good philosophy of our beloved 40th President of these United States.

Reagan was the right man, at the right hour, in the right place. And I believe it was by Divine purpose. President Reagan inspired others. He motivated millions of Americans to enter the battle for a cause that was greater than our own personal self-interest, and crucial to the survival of America and the rest of the civilized, free world. His legacy motivated me, and a great many others, to reach beyond the Grey Twilight and enter the political arena, and dedicate my life to a cause greater than self. His legacy endures, and it must.

Much damage has been done in the decades since President Reagan concluded his service as our Commander-in-Chief, especially by the likes of Bill Clinton and Barack Hussein Obama, but the legacy of President Ronald Reagan lives on! And it lives on in "We the People," citizens like you and me and President Trump, who were inspired by the great words and good deeds of President Reagan. We participated in the "Reagan Revolution," and it is now up to us to carry the banner of Conservative principles that he championed to this generation and the next. We must stand in the gap for America!

And you can start this quest by reading passages from this book to your family around the dinner table – where, as President Reagan said in his farewell address, "All great change in America begins" –and why not start this tradition tonight? Study it, and live it! Now that would be a very American thing to do!

With God's help, and your contributions to this noble effort, we can fulfill President Reagan's vision that "America's best days are yet to come!" President Trump's Administration give us this wonderful opportunity! And it all begins with a great re-discovery of the principles and oratory of this great fellow-American. It is, in the final analysis, "a re-discovery of our values and common sense," as President Reagan also said in his farewell address. Let us pray it is not too late. This is something we can achieve! "And, after all," as President Reagan said in his first inaugural address, "why shouldn't we believe that? We are Americans!"

It's Morning Again in America!

Each one of you is commissioned by history to face freedom's enemies.

~ President George W. Bush, December 7, 2001,
aboard the U.S.S. Enterprise, Norfolk, VA,
On the 60th anniversary of the Japanese sneak attack
on America at Pearl Harbor

Chapter 8

The Making of a Candidate

I thank God that I live in a country where dreams can come true, where failure sometimes is the first step to success and where success is only another form of failure if we forget what our priorities should be.

~ Harry Lloyd Hopkins, Advisor to Franklin D. Roosevelt

When William F. Buckley, Jr., ran for mayor of the city of my youth, he ran against a liberal, John V. Lindsay, and lost. That was in 1965, and a year later, Buckley wrote a book, The Unmaking of a Mayor. He lost the battle, but ultimately won the war. Through his outspoken, sometimes unpopular, championship of conservative principles, Buckley breathed life into a society that was overwhelmed by a liberal, politically correct philosophy. His was a voice that cried out in the wilderness, and millions of Americans, including yours truly, heard the call. Bill Buckley set the stage for the election of his younger brother, and one of my political heroes, James L. Buckley, to become the Conservative U.S. Senator from the State of New York following the election of 1970. And, more importantly, Buckley created a movement from a vision that culminated in the election of Ronald Reagan as the 40th President of the United States in 1980.

This is more than a chapter about what it takes to make a candidate for public office, it is about a vision and a philosophy. It is, in a broader context, a chapter about public service. And in many mays I reflect back to my race for Congress in Maryland's 5th Congressional District in the U.S. House of Representatives. And this is where my education on campaigning for public office truly began ...

When the last chapter of the history books closing the Twentieth Century are written, it is my hope they will read: There once was a time in our Nation's history, when men and women of courage took a stand for principle and honor, and, in what would have been the final days of our Republic, changed the course of American history.

We can do that! Let it be said of us that we mastered our moment, we held tight to the reigns of destiny, and we refused to settle for anything less than what was best for America.

It was with these words that I began my race for Maryland's 5th Congressional District seat in the U.S. House of Representatives in 1993. A race that would span some eighteen months, cost an untold fortune in time and money, and involve some of the most influential personalities of our time, not the least of which were Republican House Minority Leader and soon-to-be Speaker of the House, Congressman Newt Gingrich from Georgia, Liberty University Chancellor and Pastor of Thomas Road Baptist Church in Lynchburg, Virginia, Jerry Falwell, CNN Crossfire Host and Republican Candidate for President, Patrick J. Buchanan, Ralph Reed of the Christian Coalition (a man who would later become Chairman of Georgia's Republican Party, and with whom I call a friend and continue to communicate with), Congressman Dick Armey from Texas, Congressman Roscoe Bartlett from Maryland, Senator Richard Lugar from Nevada, Nixon Administration notable G. Gordon Liddy, and another candidate for office in my then-neighboring State, the Commonwealth of Virginia, Lt. Col. Ollie North (USMC, retired), who was running for the United States Senate. It would be near impossible to name them all, but my deepest gratitude goes to the hundreds of volunteers and thousands of voters who cast their votes for me and, of greater importance, the ideals and vision I championed. And, of course, the names of those with whom I met would not be complete without naming the man I fought to unseat, Congressman H. Steny Hoyer.

My campaign slogan was "Let's Make Maryland Great Again!" It was a local adaptation of a theme heralded by then-Governor Ronald Reagan some fourteen years earlier. It was also my personal statement on a campaign that began in 1976 and came to fruition in 1980.

In 1976, Ronald Reagan ran for the Republican Nomination for President. He challenged an incumbent president, Gerald Ford, and he came damn close to winning. In that season, Reagan vigorously debated his differences with Ford on the issues, including national defense, taxes, spending, government regulation, the nation's infrastructure and foreign policy. The primaries were spirited, and Reagan proved a formidable opponent, especially following his solid victories in the Deep South, starting in North Carolina. Reagan brought the issues of the day to the American people, and he forced the process out of the often-Byzantine world of back room politics. At the Republican National Convention in Kansas City, Reagan narrowly lost the nomination, gaining some 1,070 delegates to Ford's 1,197. It was the first campaign Reagan ever lost, but he was not bitter. In fact, on the final night of the convention, following President Ford's acceptance speech, a spontaneous demonstration erupted for Ronald Reagan. President Ford had no choice but to ask his challenger to address the party faithful. Reagan, in his own inimitable style, recalled an English ballad from his childhood days. "Lay me down and bleed awhile," Reagan said. "Though I am wounded, I am not slain." And as if having a vision of the year 1980, he reassured the faithful, "I shall rise and fight again."

1980 — it was a watershed year in my life! I personally met Ronald Reagan on the campaign stump in Queens, New York. He was making a tour of The Big Apple with New York

Congressman Jack Kemp. I was a graduate student at St. John's University's Graduate School of Government and Politics, in Jamaica, New York, pursuing a Graduate Certificate in International Law and Diplomacy. I was educated in one of the finest institutions of higher education in the world, and sat in classes with fellow students who held great titles in foreign lands. I was fortunate enough to have a dedicated professor who had also served as the Chairman of the New York Conservative Party, Dr. Henry Paolucci, and I learned to admire his wisdom and ongoing desire to build a better America. I met and became the friend of a U.S. Congressman from New York, Bruce Caputo, who was introduced to me by Dr. Paolucci following a debate the congressman had with Representative Herman Badillo. Congressman Caputo and I discussed the pros and cons and the finer points of his debate on that long chilly night on the St. John's campus grounds. And last, but not least, I met a beautiful young undergraduate student who would become my wife within a year.

It was a watershed in many ways, and it was a turning point in our great Nation's history. We had yet to recover from the fall of Vietnam some five years earlier, and the words of Ronald Reagan at that time in an address he gave to the VFW echoed in my ears:

> "This nation, not as fighting men, quit. Gave up for the first time and walked away not only from a war, but from an ally. There was a weakening of the will and our commitment to the cause of freedom, and it has brought a shame

on this nation more than any other single event in our nation's history. But there is no shame for the men who fought there. Those who fought in Vietnam did not lose a war, they were just not allowed to win."

He was right.

In 1980, we were in the midst of the Iran hostage crisis and, to make matters worse, the Carter Administration continued to linger on, like a cancer on the American landscape. Jimmy Carter literally managed to destroy the prospect of "peace in our time!"

I can vividly recall the deep despair in our military during the Carter years, the weakening of our National honor and the loss of morale in the ranks of our brave young fighting force. Little did I know that America would revisit such a time just over a decade later with the advent of the Clinton Administration, and a Commander in Chief who, while in office, would hold the military and its veterans in contempt, commit adultery, perjure himself, covet the infamous distinction of being the second president in our nation's history to be impeached, and bring dishonor upon the highest office in the land. And that disgrace would continue well beyond the termination of his tenure in office, with the pardoning of a multitude of convicted felons and drug peddlers, and a seemingly endless trail of corruption that would permeate the national landscape.

But 1980 heralded a brief shining moment in America's history. We would elect perhaps the greatest president in my lifetime, Ronald Reagan, who would fulfill his rendezvous with destiny.

A half-year later, on March 30, 1981, I would be in Congressman Bruce Caputo's office in New York City, turning down a position to work on his campaign staff in his bid to oust freshman Senator Daniel Patrick Moynihan, and waiting to hear the fate of President Ronald Reagan, who was just wounded in an assassination attempt in Washington, D.C. As I recall, Caputo was initially convinced that the president had been assassinated, and I sat with him as he repeatedly called the White House switchboard, only to receive no answer.

Then came the news: President Reagan was alive! We breathed a deep sigh of relief. And America began her longest military and economic peacetime expansion in history. Reagan renewed the Spirit of America, and on a lonely parade field at Fort Bragg, North Carolina, "Home of the XVIII Airborne Corps and the 82d Airborne Division," in July of 1981, I was honored by Secretary of the Army John O. Marsh, when he administered my oath of office and bestowed upon me my commission as an Infantry Officer in the United States Army. I became an Officer when President Reagan was Commander in Chief, and the whole world seemed a bit better off, and I knew for a fact that America's military was on the road to recovery. And so it was.

In less than a month, Second Lieutenant Moroz would marry the former Denise Elizabeth Perrone, and both would spend their honeymoon at the "Home of the Infantry," beautiful Fort Benning, Georgia. In fact, we spent a good part of our first full day married voluntarily running laps around the Airborne track.

It was truly the best of times!

Little did I ever envision Jimmy Carter would not be the worst president in the history of the republic. That title was fought over by his Democrat successor to the White House, Bill Clinton, who was impeached by the U.S. House of Representatives and narrowly escaped removal by the U.S. Senate. But revisionists of history note that period of moral decay with fondness. And if that was not bad enough, along came the unvetted junior senator from Illinois, Barack Hussein Obama.

Americans longed for a change for the better, a time of Hope and Change." Unfortunately, that well-intentioned quest has brought us to a point not unlike the one Great Britain was at just before the Second World War. We chose a trusting naive, appeasement-minded path, the consequences of which are a wrecked economy with some $20 trillion in national debt, a dangerously weakened military, the likes of which we have not had since before the Second World War, and America's honor left trampled and spat upon in the deepening quagmire.

And so it is! And despite the re-birth of America during the Reagan Administration, America is worse off now than ever before in our history!

Great Britain lost her ability to deter war in the late 1930's; today we find ourselves in a similar position, thanks in great part to the Obama legacy. Fortunately for Great Britain in World War II, America was waiting in the wings and came to the rescue. Unfortunately for America, no superpower is waiting in the wings to come to our rescue.

To be accurate, history must charge Barack Hussein Obama with having greatly contributed to the loss of America's ability to deter war. In fact, he enabled and empowered America's enemies! And I do not make that charge lightly!

But I do not believe all is lost! I believe America is in the midst of a great awakening! I witnessed such during the Reagan Revolution, and I tried to emulate that campaign in a small but meaningful way in my race for Congress.

Congress was once the key to placing a president's tremendous power in check, at least it was before the advent of establishment Republican politicians who entered Congressional leadership posts after the Reagan era and found it most advantageous for themselves to go along with a president of the opposing party. Congress abrogated its constitutional duty to the American people under Obama, as did the Judiciary. It is important to note a few things about Congress, despite what some may say. Congress exists as a co-equal branch of government with the Executive and Judicial. It is responsible for making the laws. It is as important as the Executive and Judiciary Branches in the scheme of the Constitution. And although more than 11,000 people, most of who were men, have served in both the House and Senate of the Congress since the signing of the Constitution, each member has a critical role to play in our republic. Consequently, the American public has a vital duty to fulfill when it votes for any candidate to hold an office of such high public trust.

I learned many lessons from my campaign for Congress. And a lot about campaigning, a great deal about the problems Americans face in our day to day lives, and perhaps more than I care to know about the machinery of government and the people who operate that machinery. I shook tens of thousands of hands, addressed more audiences than I can remember (audiences that included Senators Richard Lugar and Phil Gramm, Congressmen Dick Armey and Roscoe Bartlett, and a host of other political notables), and would like to enthusiastically say, I'd do it all again, but I would be lying. It was difficult, personally and professionally, and it was a great deal less enjoyable than one might first imagine.

This is not to say that there was no enjoyment. In fact, I had many enjoyable and memorable moments! Being introduced to an enthusiastic crowd of thousands of patriotic Americans by Dr. Jerry Falwell was an incredible experience. Sharing an afternoon with then-House Minority Leader Newt Gingrich at his office in the Capitol, and discussing what he feared was the "inevitable nationalization and destruction of our healthcare system by Hillary Clinton," was historic! Throwing out the opening pitch at the home game of the minor league Bowie Baysox baseball team (during the major league baseball strike of 1994, to a sold-out hometown crowd, while my opponent, Cong. Steny Hoyer, was in the stands, and the scoreboard repeatedly spelled out "M-O-R-O-Z for Congress, Let's Make Maryland Great Again!") was phenomenal! [by the way, I did throw a strike—my son witnessed that]. And having the trust of so many thousands of citizens who voted for me was both an emotional and humbling experience.

The '94 campaign was unique in the annals of American political history. The House of Representatives had been in the hands of the Democrats for some 40 years, and Newt Gingrich had pledged to make a "Contract with America" and take back the House. And so he did.

In the D.C. metropolitan area, where my congressional district was located, we had a hodgepodge of candidates and philosophies. In Virginia, which bordered my district to the south, we had Ollie North running for the United States Senate (I fondly recall walking through an Army barracks at Fort Bragg, N.C., in the summer of '87, during which time I heard the roar of cheers by fellow-military personnel who were applauding Lt. Col. North's testimony before a hostile Democrat committee hearing on Capitol Hill). I admire Ollie for his patriotism, his loyalty to the president, and his refusal to abandon the contras, who were fighting for the cause of freedom against a Communist foothold on the shores of our own hemisphere in Nicaragua (despite the fact that a liberal Congress at the time abandoned freedom fighters in the field and lacked the courage to take a stand). The fact we had military backgrounds in common, amongst a great many other things, prompted one Maryland newspaper, The Laurel Leader, to headline a story on me in its issue of February 24,

1994, and dub the article, and by reference me, "The Ollie North of District 5." I accepted it as a compliment!

In Washington, D.C., which bordered my district to the west, we had Marion Barry running for Mayor (enough said on that subject). And in Maryland, we had former U.S. Senator from Tennessee Bill Brock running for the U.S. Senate again, only this time from Maryland! Bill and I had several conversations about the Maryland Republican Party. And in the middle of all that, in a not so tiny, diverse district, we had yours truly, running to replace the fourth ranking liberal Democrat in the U.S. House of Representatives, Steny Hoyer. It was an interesting battleground, the likes of which I never encountered in the military!

The Laurel Leader article comparing me to Lt. Col. Ollie North spelled out several political truths I had encountered in my race. One such truth was the lack of support, if not downright opposition I received from the state GOP leadership. Others who supported my campaign and also ran for the same seat in years gone by also observed this. I was apparently too far to the right, and I was not willing enough to compromise on my positions. As the writer of the article, Elizabeth Lean, observed, "Moroz…is ignoring advice to run a 'two-pronged campaign' that would showcase his conservatism to the 'hard-core hunters' of the district's southern portion but soft-pedal his anti-abortion stand and other issues in more urban Prince George's."

I was an oddity for the Washington, D.C.-area press corps. I never hid from the issues! And much to the dismay of many

Republican campaign advisers, I spelled out exactly where I stood on virtually every issue. And I was always willing to debate my positions with anyone who might challenge them. I admire any man who takes a position and has the courage to defend that position with reason and integrity.

Annapolis, Maryland's *The Capital* newspaper, jumped on my entering the race for Congress in its August 12, 1993, edition as follows:

Moroz Candidacy

The liberals are coming! The liberals are coming! Likening himself to Paul Revere and arguing that the nation can indeed legislate morality, a conservative Republican from Churchton has entered the 1994 5th Congressional District race.

Harold R. "Hal" Moroz, of Churchton, announced his candidacy July 30 at the Riverdale Baptist Church in Upper Marlboro, where he was introduced and endorsed by the Rev. Jerry Falwell, a conservative televangelist and founder of the Moral Majority.

The 5th District seat is now held by Rep. Steny Hoyer of Prince George's County, the fourth-ranking Democrat in the House of Representatives. It comprises southern Prince George's and Calvert, St. Mary's and Charles counties and includes the southern third of Anne Arundel...

"Together, we can stop this insanity of legislating immorality and make Maryland great again," the pro-death penalty, anti-abortion candidate said at his campaign announcement.

"Make no mistake, we are at war! This time, the war is being waged against our children, our economy, our military, and our cultural heritage—this war is being waged by President Clinton and his pals like Steny Hoyer in the Congress."...

A sampling of his positions:

- Death penalty for convicted murderers.
- English as the official national language.
- Prayer in public schools.
- Reduction in federal spending and a balanced budget.
- Overturning the 1977 Panama Canal Treaty.
- Anti-abortion.
- Against tax increases of any kind.
- Supports a ban on homosexuals serving in the military.
- Against statehood for the District of Columbia.

Despite the criticisms of newspapers and reporters that inaccurately reflect the words and positions of candidates, *The*

Capital was correct and right on point with regard to my stand on those issues!

The Voice of Southern Maryland, another newspaper, recorded my debut as follows on the front page of its August 17, 1993, issue:

Republican Announces Challenge to Hogan with Falwell Backing

At Upper Marlboro, Maryland, Friday night (July 30th) at the River-dale Baptist Church the Rev. Jerry Falwell announced and introduced his "clear choice" to unseat the incumbent Democrat Steny Hoyer in Maryland's 5th Congressional District in '94.

To an audience of more than 500 at his "Wake Up America" conference, Falwell introduced Anne Arundel-based Republican candidate for congress Harold R. "Hal" Moroz as "an example of the principled, courageous leadership our Congress needs to confront the devastating initiative of the Clinton Administration."

"Hal Moroz is a former airborne-Infantry officer who served our Nation with great distinction in the United States Army," Falwell said, "and he was a university professor of history and government—he has all the credentials to serve the interests of Maryland and our nation in the United States Congress."

"He's against raising your taxes; he's for balancing the budget and reducing the national debt; he's against homosexuals in our military; he's for prayer in our nation's schools; he's against abortion on demand; he's for capital punishment; and he's against the Clinton agenda to undermine our families, our military and the economy," declared Falwell as he introduced the candidate. "Hal Moroz is batting a thousand with me!"

As the first speaker of the evening, Candidate Moroz introduced his "Let's Make Maryland Great Again" theme and challenged the audience to "make a difference in their own communities."...

Since filing as a Republican candidate for Maryland's 5th Congressional District seat in the U.S. House of Representatives on April 15 of this year, Candidate Moroz has been traveling throughout his district addressing civic groups and concerned citizens about the need for change in Congress. Stressing family values, the economy and Maryland's future, Hal Moroz' campaign includes pledges to earmark 10% of his congressional salary—starting on the first day in office—to be returned to the U.S.

Treasury for the specific purpose of debt reduction, and distributing another 15% of his salary to his church...

The Hogan mentioned in *The Voice* article headline was a reference to the son of Larry Hogan, Sr., a former Maryland "Republican" Congressman who aggressively attacked President Nixon during the Watergate scandal, and publicly joined ranks with the liberal Democrats in their unsuccessful attempt to impeach the president in 1974. Hogan was a favorite of the state party leadership because of his father, and the fact he had previously run against Hoyer, but lost. Hogan was originally scheduled to debate me in a Republican forum attended by Senator Richard Lugar from Nevada. Hogan wound up not showing, and eventually never did formally enter the race.

My campaign was mentioned in many forums across Maryland and the United States. Notable forums, which resulted in various reviews (depending on the political persuasion of the reviewers), included The Washington Post, The Washington Times, the nationally syndicated G. Gordon Liddy Radio Program, the nationally televised Old Time Gospel Hour, and the list of programs and newspapers goes on and on. Keeping track of the comments about the campaign and me was too overwhelming a task for one lean campaign organization to accomplish. Nevertheless, I did grow to understand and appreciate the frustrations of other candidates who objected to manufactured "quotes" and comments unfairly taken out of context. Many savvy media watchers told me, "It goes along with the territory." And so it did.

As I previously hinted, I was not the sweetheart of the Maryland Republican Party leadership. My campaign style was confrontational and to the point. I was an outsider, much like Donald Trump. My campaign was unconventional in many ways, and that fact was pointed out by reporter Eva Munk of the Capital News Service, when she wrote an article on my campaign entitled, "Welcome to the World of a Guerrilla Candidate." I wanted the voters to know the issues and where all the candidates stood, including myself! I often criticized what I saw as the Maryland Republican Party's liberal leanings, and its failure to take a position on any controversial issue. Those liberal leanings and its method of operation no doubt contributed to its many defeats. It was the primary reason why the last Republican Governor to be elected in Maryland was Spiro T. Agnew. My contention was that the liberals would be more inclined to vote for the Democrats than Republicans who were merely imitating the Democrats. Why not vote for the real thing? Conservatives, Pro-Lifers, Libertarians, and Republicans needed a real alternative to the liberal choices offered by both of the major parties in that state, and they just were not getting it from the Maryland Republican Party.

I attempted to offer a clear choice for the voters, but, in many ways, the lack of party support (against a Democrat who had a campaign war chest that exceeded $2 million from the beginning) was an insurmountable battle for me. Unlike Donald Trump, I did not have the money to go it alone. The party apparatus, in my opinion, would rather lose than support a conservative Republican. And so they did.

To make a long story short, I lost the race for Congress. And, to be honest, I felt devastated by the outcome. I am competitive by nature, and "losing" is not in my vocabulary. The stakes were too high, and the issues too great, for me to think anything other than victory, and I carried the burden of satisfying the prayers of those who supported my campaign with their time, their money, their reputations, and their votes! I am reminded of a conversation that took place between Joseph G. Cannon, William McKinley, and Benjamin Butterworth in 1890, following the defeat of all three men in their bids for re-election to the U.S. House of Representatives. They had met in Chicago following the election, and over dinner, McKinley and Butterworth remarked about how glad they were over the results of the election. They gleefully commented about all the time they could now devote to their private lives. "Oh, hell boys!" replied Cannon, "tell that to the marines. There's no use for us to lie to one another! It hurts, and it hurts damned bad!" And so it did!

Even today, I cringe when I hear citizens mock those with the courage to enter the political arena, even when it is directed at members of the opposition party. I have witnessed this form of mockery intensely on social media.

But as for my race, in a small but meaningful way, a message was delivered to the citizens of Maryland and America. I am convinced it was a fight worth waging! Seeds were planted during that election. Seeds that may very well grow and bear fruit in the form of a new birth of Republican values in Maryland, and other troubled states, in the not so distant future. A battle was lost, but the war continues, and the Quest endures!

I believe in many ways my campaign set the stage for Bob Erlich to attain the governorship of Maryland in 2003, and Larry Hogan after him in 2015. Yes, it was the same Larry Hogan I met some 20 years before.

People often ask me, "What makes you a Republican?"

"The belief that people, not government, can best solve the problems we face," I most often reply. "Conservative Republicans trust God and America's citizens, liberal Democrats trust government." And it is more than that. I am a Conservative-Republican because it is the political philosophy of smaller government, lower-taxes, peace through strength, pro-life, states rights, traditional family values, and a limited government that operates in the strict limits of the express words of the Constitution, that includes a healthy respect for the right of American citizens to keep and bear arms! President Reagan fought hard to make it that way, and we have a duty to keep this the philosophy of the Republican Party, the Party of Reagan!

With that said, I leave the question of what it takes to make a Congressman or a President for that matter in your hands.

I stand by the proposition that "We the people" can improve our system of government and our way of life, not our government or an elite media that promotes political correctness like torrential rains promote floods. You know what makes a good Congressman and a good President, and I trust you will make that known this coming election! I hope this colloquy helps you to make an informed decision the next time you cast your vote for the candidate of your choice.

My race for Congress made me a better American and a better person. For those reasons, it was personally very rewarding. It made me knowledgeable of the plight, concerns and dreams of average Americans in our community, and more knowledgeable about the political process in America, despite what I thought I knew because of my many years of teaching American History and Government. Experience truly is the best educator. And the race also made me sympathetic to all those brave souls who step beyond the Grey Twilight, and dwell in the not-so-brilliant sunshine of the political arena (regardless of their political party), and suffer defeat.

I recall an English ballad that President Reagan spoke about from his childhood days. "Lay me down and bleed awhile," Reagan said. "Though I am wounded, I am not slain." And as if having a vision of the future, he reassured the faithful, "I shall rise and fight again." And so it shall be.

It's Morning Again in America!

I do not believe in a fate that will fall on us no matter what we do. I do believe in a fate that will fall on us if we do nothing. So, with all the creative energy at our command, let us begin an era of national renewal. Let us renew our determination, our courage, and our strength. And let us renew our faith and our hope. We have every right to dream heroic dreams.

~ President Ronald Reagan, January 20, 1981

If you can bear to hear the truth you've spoken
Twisted by knaves to make a trap for fools,
Or watch the things you gave your life to, broken,
And stoop and build'em up with worn-out tools;

If you can make one heap of all your winnings
And risk it on one turn of pitch-and-toss,
And lose, and start again at your beginnings,
And never breathe a word about your loss:

If you can force your heart and nerve and sinew
To serve your turn long after they are gone,
And so hold on when there is nothing in you
Except the Will which says to them: "Hold on!"

If you can talk with crowds and keep your virtue,
Or walk with Kings---nor lose the common touch,
If neither foes nor loving friends can hurt you,
If all men count with you, but none too much:
If you can fill the unforgiving minute
With sixty seconds' worth of distance run,
Yours is the Earth and everything that's in it,
And---which is more---you'll be a Man, my son!

~ Rudyard Kipling

Above: Author Commissioned a 2d Lieutenant, July 1981
Below: Author serving as a Captain detailed for the re-interment of a
WW II soldier KIA in Europe *(photos courtesy U.S. Army)*

The Author in the service of his country as a
U.S. Army Airborne Infantry officer *(photos courtesy U.S. Army)*

Author literally running for Maryland's 5th Congressional District
seat in the U.S. House of Representatives, 1994

The Author declaring his candidacy for Maryland's 5th Congressional
District seat in the U.S. House of Representatives, 1993
(photo courtesy The Calvert Recorder)

Above: Author & family (wife Denise, son, William, & daughter, Heather)
with friend Dr. Jerry Falwell, 1993.
Below: Author with then-House Minority Leader Newt Gingrich, R-GA,
Sep. 1993 *(Photo courtesy U.S. House of Representatives)*

Above: Author is sworn in as a Judge in the State of Georgia, Dec. 2000
(photo courtesy Camden County, GA)
Below: Author with wife Denise in Andersonville, Georgia, 2003.

Above; Author as a Judge tours the Andersonville, Georgia
Historic CSA POW Camp & Cemetery, 2003.
Below: Author & wife Denise, with friend, Dr. Charles Stanley, 2012.

On-Air Talk Radio with friend Audrey Russo (above) &
Paul & Vickie Hafer & the WECC Lighthouse family (below)

Judge Hal Moroz speaks on the 10 Commandments as the foundation of America's civil and criminal codes at WECC The Lighthouse, St. Marys, Georgia, 2004 (*Photo courtesy Paul Hafer*)

Eldorado

Gaily bedight,
A gallant knight,
In sunshine and in shadow,
Had journeyed long,
Singing a song,
In search of Eldorado.

But he grew old-
This knight so bold-
And o'er his heart a shadow
Fell as he found
No spot of ground
That looked like Eldorado.

And, as his strength
Failed him at length,
He met a pilgrim shadow-
"Shadow," said he,
"Where can it be-
This land of Eldorado?"

"Over the Mountains
Of the Moon,
Down the Valley of the Shadow,
Ride, boldly ride,"
The shade replied-
"If you seek for Eldorado!"

~ Edgar Allan Poe

Chapter 9

Airborne

There should be no fear – we are protected, and we will always be protected. We will be protected by the great men and women of our military and law enforcement and, most importantly, we are protected by God.

~ President Donald Trump, January 20, 2017

Discourage vice in every shape, and impress upon the mind of every man, from first to the lowest, the importance of the cause, and what it is they are contending for.

~ General George Washington, November 10, 1775

Airborne! A word. A shout. A way of life! And fifteen years following America's last official involvement in the

Vietnam War, I found myself in Southeast Asia, an Airborne Captain of Infantry, jumping out of a perfectly good helicopter, along with members of Thailand's elite Special Forces Group, some eleven-hundred feet above a landscape covered by jungle and an occasional rice paddy.

It was July, and a particularly hot and humid day as I recall. We were based in Lop Buri, a remote village in the jungle about a hundred miles north of Bangkok. We boarded our helicopters, old Hueys, workhorses during the Vietnam War, door guns intact, bearing full combat gear, and our parachutes, of course. The pilots headed east. We passed along an ancient land and approached the Mekong River, and it brought back many images I had seen and heard about. A time when the blood of brave young Americans was spilled liberally over this land, and we left in such a hurry that fellow soldiers were left behind to rot in prison camps in places without names just a few clicks away.

I could see the foothills of the Himalayas loom in the distance as we traversed vast expanses of jungle. Soon it was time to hook-up our parachute static lines and stand in the door of the chopper. As we jumped, the parachutes would be yanked from their pouches by a line of chord fastened to the helicopter.

Airborne soldiers are trained to trust their equipment and training. You stand in the door, legs outstretched, and leap from the chopper's landing skid, then you count to four. One thousand, two thousand, three thousand, four thousand, and whoosh, your chute is deployed. It's all in the training. And if that doesn't work, you pop your reserve chute positioned on your waist. You learn to trust your equipment and training. You have little other choice.

Today was different. The conditions were just right. During my military career, I had jumped out of propeller airplanes, jets, helicopters, even hot air balloons, but the conditions today were very good. The wind was calm, the sky was clear, it seemed a little less oppressively hot than usual, and we were in excellent spirits.

As I exited the chopper, my chute deployed without a hitch. I surveyed the land, found the direction of the wind, and headed into it. I spotted a landing point amidst the triple canopy jungle, a sparse patch of ground as a drop zone, which just happened to be an old rice paddy.

I executed a PLF (Parachute Landing Fall) into the ancient rice paddy. To my surprise, the water was deep! Water buffaloes loomed in the distance. Not much time to think about anything else but the mission, but it was hot and incredibly humid. I had spent previous years in Georgia, running up and down tank trails in 100-plus degree (F) weather, but nothing prepared me for this type of climate. In reflection, the 1990 United States Marine Corps Marathon, in Washington, D.C., where I finished the Olympic distance of 26 miles 385 yards with a time of 4 hours, 13 minutes, and 4 seconds, seemed like a walk in the park when compared to a day in the field during my earlier tour of duty in Thailand. I felt as if I carried the weight of the world on my back!

It was a mere day in a career, and when I think back to that day, and others like it, I am reminded of the men and woman who live similar days even today as I write—men who walk the demilitarized zone in Korea, with weapons locked and loaded; men who search caves in far-off lands, seeking intelligence on an elusive and cowardly enemy, in what our national military leaders call the Global War Against Terrorism (GWAT); and the men and woman of the Army, Navy, Air Force and Marines who do the work of defending this great Nation each and every minute, of each and every day. They perform their duties in the finest traditions of Roman Honor.

Military service is an honor and a privilege. It taught me well about life and death. And I thank God every day for having given me the opportunity to serve in Washington's Army. It prepared me well for the challenges of life and continued service to my Nation and the cause we pursue.

But I ponder the negative impact Obama and the eight years of his season had on our military, and I fear for our service men and women, and those who were wounded in battle. Before January 20, 2017, our military civilian leadership never served in uniform. Like Obama, they demeaned military service as a last resort for society's outcasts. Nothing could be further from the truth!

President Trump, on the other hand, has nothing but respect for our military and its role in the preservation of the republic. He understands the mission of our military is to win wars, and in times of peace deter war. This was President

Reagan's doctrine of Peace through Strength. It works! But a great deal of damage has been done.

Obama and his allies sanitized the military branches with their politically correct visions of how the world should be, never realizing or appreciating the sacrifice endured by our men and women in uniform and their families. To paraphrase Obama's Vice President, "Nothing is more important to our military than the inclusion of our transgendered community." A pronouncement shared by Obama's hapless Secretary of Defense. What utter non-sense! They have absolutely no idea of what it takes to keep a nation free ... or to walk a post on the walls of this bright shining city on a hill!

Nevertheless, I trust President Trump, and we who propelled him through the primaries and into office! America's once "Silent Majority" has waking up to the utter incompetence and stupidity of our Establishment "leadership," and I trust genuine positive change is in the air!

Throughout my time in the uniform of our country, I developed a philosophy about service, our men and women in uniform, and the military and civilian leadership required to sustain the force and keep America's military might second to none. I believe President Trump shares that philosophy. It is based upon the time-tested philosophies of Julius Caesar, Napoleon, Washington, Andrew Jackson, Lee, Eisenhower, MacArthur, and lesser-known leaders I had the great privilege of serving under and learning from.

The philosophy of these American heroes inspires me. As you no doubt noticed, the chapters of this book begin with quotes: Words of inspiration and truth from the pages of history. They complement the chapters and reinforce the values and beliefs of our cause. I trust they will inspire you as well, and remind us all of the price that has been paid, lest we forget.

It's Morning Again in America!

War is an ugly thing, but not the ugliest of things; the decayed and degraded state of moral and patriotic feeling which thinks that nothing is worth war is much worse. A man who has nothing for which he is willing to fight; nothing he cares about more than his own personal safety, is a miserable creature who has no chance of being free, unless made and kept so by the exertions of better men than himself.

~ John Stuart Mill

Chapter 10

Lex Est Arma Regum

The courts must declare the sense of the law; and if they should be disposed to exercise WILL instead of JUDGMENT, the consequence would be the substitution of their pleasure to that of the legislative body.

~ The Federalist No. 78 (Alexander Hamilton)

It is, emphatically, the province and duty of the judicial department to say what the law is.

~ Chief Justice John Marshall,
Marbury v. Madison, 5 U.S. 137, 177 (1803).

"...I do so solemnly swear to support and defend the Constitution of the United States!"

It was with this closing, with my left hand on the Bible and right hand raised, that I accepted my appointment and concluded my oath as a new Judge in the Great State of Georgia on December 21st, 2000. It was an oath not unlike the one I was administered two decades earlier as a newly commissioned Second Lieutenant of Infantry in the United States Army by Secretary of the Army John O. Marsh on a sun-scorched parade field at Fort Bragg, North Carolina. And it was an oath I would honor with the same level of intensity, pledging my life, my fortune and my sacred honor to achieving its purposes. And so it was.

It was a bright October morning in St. Marys, Georgia. October 12th, 2000, to be exact, and Chief Magistrate-elect Harvey L. Fry of the Magistrate Court of Camden County, Georgia, had invited me and Dar Hendrickson, a career law enforcement officer, to lunch at Borrell Creek in beautiful St. Marys. The moment was somber, because earlier that day global terrorists struck the U.S.S. Cole in the Middle East, killing seventeen brave young Americans. It was only a matter of time before the terrorists would cross that great expanse of ocean and strike a blow to the heart of America at the World Trade Center, in New York City's financial district, and the Pentagon itself.

Judge Fry, a career naval officer who retired in the South, had won a decisive election victory in the once-tranquil coastal hamlet of Camden County, Georgia. He witnessed firsthand the rapid growth of a sleepy county of just a few thousand to a thriving community of some 50,000 citizens. It deserves noting that the entire population of Georgia at the time of the first census in 1790 was 82,548. Times were changing, and so were the demands on this judge and the court he led.

This October meeting with Judge Fry was an invitation to join the judicial branch. He was building a team to help administer justice in a small corner of America—Camden County to be exact, and he had a plan.

Judge Fry had two requirements for the job (the Georgia Code articulates all the other requirements for serving as a Magistrate Judge). They were simple and forthright, clear and unambiguous.

"Obey the Law, and use common sense," he said. That was it! Now when have you heard advice like that in government? Obey the Law and use common sense! It sounds revolutionary today, doesn't it?

Camden County's Magistrate Court Judges would administer justice in a fair and impartial manner, avoiding any appearance of impropriety, and in a way that would honorably serve the interests of the Law and the American citizens who placed such great trust and confidence in us. And so we would!

It seemed like a blink of an eye, that is, the period between October 12th and December 21st. My involvement in the Presidential Election and the constitutional crisis that followed no doubt contributed to the swift passage of time. Nevertheless, the process of confirming my judgeship went on without a hitch. Judge Fry presented my credentials to the Brunswick Circuit Superior Court Judges, who approved and confirmed my nomination, and I received my Commission as a Judge of the Magistrate Court of Camden County from the Governor of the Great State of Georgia.

New Year's Day 2001 brought forth a flurry of commitments and opportunities. I hit the ground running as a judge on January 2nd, hearing case after case, and getting my feet wet as a judge, instead of being the lawyer who made arguments to the judge during so many of the preceding years. I was also under consideration for several positions in the incoming Bush Administration, including that of a federal judgeship.

Despite being supported for a post in the Bush Administration by my local Congressman, Republican Jack Kingston, the Georgia Republican Party First Congressional District Committee's Chairman, Dr. James H. Burnham, and other political, judicial, and business leaders in the State of Georgia, the prospects of a federal judgeship in the Great State of Georgia were dim. Both of Georgia's U.S. Senators are Democrats (traditionally, judicial nominees are supported by both senators of their home state), and I had several strikes against me (at least in the eyes of local and national Democrats). I have been a Registered Republican since I was old enough to vote (and voted for Ronald Reagan over Gerald Ford in the Primary, and Gerald Ford over Jimmy Carter in the '76 Presidential Election). I have also been a card-carrying member of the Federalist Society since the early 90's (a fact I disclosed on my federal judgeship paperwork, when asked to disclose what organizations I held membership in). The Federalist Society for Law and Public Policy Studies is a group of conservatives and libertarians interested in the current state of the legal order. It is founded on the principles that the state exists to preserve freedom, that the separation of governmental powers is central to our Constitution, and that it is emphatically the province and duty of the judiciary to say what the law is, not what it should be. As a side note, Ted Olson and Robert Bork are also members of the Federalist Society.

To make matters worse, nationally, Senator Jim Jeffords of Vermont turned his back on the Republican Party after it supported him for re-election in 2000. He quit the Republican Party on May 24, 2001 — knowing full well that it would turn control of the U.S. Senate over to the Democrats. His act, which earned him the dubious title of "Senator Turncoat" on Capitol Hill, effectively removed conservative Republican Orrin Hatch of Utah as Chair of the powerful Senate Judiciary Committee, and placed liberal Democrat Patrick Leahy of Vermont at the helm. The prospects of conservative Bush nominees being confirmed to administration positions, including posts in the federal judiciary, was doubtful at best and, in fact, ultimately ground such confirmations to a halt. Gridlock returned to Washington, D.C., thanks in great part to a senator who effectively blocked any Republican opposition to his senate seat by posing as a "Republican" candidate during the election, and the Democrat majority in the Senate he helped to create.

I won't even address the implications of my having supported the Bush-Cheney legal efforts in post-election Florida or being a member of the Federalist Society! Even to the casual observer, they become self-evident.

Locally, my opposition to the way the Georgia flag was changed in January 2001 would not go unnoticed. The old Georgia flag was replaced by an elite few, led by Georgia's Governor, Roy Barnes, and his floor leader, our local representative in the Georgia House, Charlie Smith, Jr., both liberal Democrats. The two, after assuring voters no such move to replace the flag would take place in 2001, secretly unveiled their new flag, affectionately called the "Barnes-Smith Flag" by locals, and shoved it down the throats of the citizens of Georgia, without so much as an opportunity to debate the issue or consider alternates. It was a shameful return to the good ol' boy, back door, smoke-filled rooms days of the past. The new flag was foisted by the Democrats in a matter of days, and done so hastily that it may have very well violated federal law in the process, as the new Georgia flag placed the United States flag in an inferior position on its field of blue.

The scene was much like the despicable way Gov. Nikki Haley (R-SC) succumbed to the shouts of the mob to take down the Confederate Battle flag from its place of honor on the grounds of the South Carolina state capital.

My willingness to speak out on the issues of the day may very well have cost me an opportunity to serve on the federal judiciary, but such is the price we pay whenever we take a stand. And taking such stands is the least one can do to honor the memories of our Founding Fathers, who pledged their lives, their fortunes, and their sacred honor to create the climate for the freedoms we now so easily take for granted.

I am encouraged by the few who take stands on the issues of our, especially in the judiciary. I applaud the stance of Kentucky Court Clerk Kim Davis in taking a stand for her First Amendment rights and refusing to yield and accept the Supreme Court's blatant disregard for Western Civilization's definition of Marriage and 5,000 years of history. By standing up for her constitutional rights, Ms. Davis stood up for ours as well. I encourage all who would read these words to read Justice Antonin Scalia's scathing dissent of the Supreme Court's decision in *Obergefell v. Hodges*.

Chief Justice Roy S. Moore of the Great State of Alabama is another such example. In 1997, as an appointed Circuit Judge of the Sixteenth Judicial Circuit in Etowah County, Judge Moore came under heavy fire by the ACLU and others for his display of the Ten Commandments in his courtroom. It was but one of the many ongoing assaults on prayer and the mere mention of God in public places. And they have gotten much worse under the regime of Barack Hussein Obama.

Moore, a veteran of the Army and company commander in Vietnam, refused to yield to the rabid voices of moral relativism and political correctness that demanded the cornerstone of all Western Civilization civil and criminal codes (i.e., thou shalt not kill, thou shalt not commit adultery, thou shalt not steal, thou shalt not bear false witness against thy neighbor, etc.) be removed from our Courts of Law. Incredible! What law should we apply? And what will they demand next? The removal of the Bibles upon which judges take their oaths of office? Or how about preventing another American president from using a Bible to take his oath of office at the Capitol? By the way, the Bible President Bush placed his hand upon to take the oath of office was the same used by his father, and President George Washington before him!

The bright ray of hope in Judge Moore's case was that the good citizens of Alabama recognized and rewarded the judge's courage and commitment to moral leadership by repeatedly electing him Chief Justice of the Alabama Supreme Court.

When I became a lawyer, I was given a ring. I wear it still. The ring is a simple band of gold, inscribed with a Latin maxim, "Lex Est Arma Regum," meaning, "Law is the Arm of the King." The ring was commissioned by King James of England—the same King James who commissioned the 1611 King James Version of the Bible. The bearers of these rings were the representative arms of the law and the King. The ring was historically bestowed on knights of the realm who served the cause of justice, law and order. It was part of an oath to support and defend the law. Bestowed upon these trusted knights was the right to bear arms, and the power to meet justice. They maintained a duty and a trust that endures even to the present day.

A lawyer friend of mine once told me he'd gladly pay to see my Senate confirmation hearing, if one were ever held. "It would make the Bork hearing look like a tea party," he said. I disagree.

Regardless, in April 2001, while a sitting judge on the Magistrate Court of Camden County, I would undergo consideration for a federal judgeship in the U.S. District Court for the Northern District of Illinois, specifically as the full-time United States Magistrate Judge in Chicago (and shortly thereafter for a vacancy in the U.S. District Court for the Middle District of Florida). The process involved volumes of paperwork and disclosures of all kinds. I had flashbacks to Army life and the frequent moves we made from one post to another, and uprooting our children from one school to another. In the end, if duty called, even if it meant moving to Chicago, we would answer that call. We would move to the sound of the cannon. We were prepared to do our part to support the Bush agenda. Still, if we moved, I would leave my heart in Georgia. For this family, Georgia will always be home.

On June 7, 2001, the Chairman of the federal judgeship selection panel formally notified me that I was not selected for the Chicago position (as well as with the Florida position later in time). With mixed emotions, and a sigh of relief, we accepted the decision. And life went on for the Moroz Family in beautiful Georgia, and in two short years I would become the Chief Judge of the City of St. Marys, Georgia, and go on to appoint the first woman to become a judge in the history of

America's second oldest city! That Judge, Kathe Loeffler, now serves of the Chief Judge of that beautiful coastal Georgia city.

Being a judge is a great honor and a distinct privilege, whether on the state or federal level. It is also a unique experience, which entails great responsibility. It is quite different from my role as a lawyer, although the two serve as officers of the court. A judge, unlike a lawyer, cannot be an advocate for either party in the courtroom. Decisions are made based on the facts and the law. However, with the precedent set by the Roberts Supreme Court in *Obergefell v. Hodges* and *King v. Burwell*, judges are no longer confided to that ideal, and instead have been given licenses to rewrite the laws of the legislature and substitute their will for the law. The Roberts Supreme Court, I predict, will go down in history as "The Dred Scott[10] Supreme Court of the 21st Century."

Even with the above said, there still rages a great debate in the modern judiciary. Judges are divided on the limits of their power and their roles on the bench. Many believe their job is to interpret the law in an innovative fashion, even creating laws at times, to dispense a brand of justice that suits popular opinion or their good pleasure. It is the type of jurisprudence that was exercised by the United States Supreme Court in 2015, and by the Florida Supreme Court in November and December of 2000. I disagree with that form of judicial activism. It is emphatically the province and duty of the judiciary to say what the law is, not what it should be. If

---

[10] *Dred Scott v. Sandford*, 60 U.S. 393 (1857), was a landmark decision by the U.S. Supreme Court that held blacks in America were not citizens, and had no standing in federal court to file lawsuits.

judges want to make laws, let them run for legislative office. Judges are there to interpret the law, nothing more and nothing less. And that in itself is an awesome task.

Judges hold positions of great trust and power. The latter must be exercised wisely, using great restraint, and with exceeding sound judgment. To wield that sword to satisfy his or her personal whims or desires, I believe, is a breach of duty and the public trust placed in that individual, and an act which is in diametrical opposition to the intent of our Founding Fathers when they established the judiciary under our Constitution.

Justice Benjamin Cardozo said it best in 1921, when he addressed the debate even as it raged in his own time:

> The Judge, even when he is free, is still not wholly free. He is not to innovate at pleasure. He is not a knight-errant, roaming at will in pursuit of his own ideal of beauty or of goodness. He is to draw his inspiration from consecrated principles. He is not to yield to spasmodic sentiment, to vague and unregulated benevolence. He is to exercise a discretion informed by tradition, methodized by analogy, disciplined by system, and subordinated to "the primordial necessity of order in the social life." Wide enough in all conscience is the field of discretion that remains.

Unfortunately, the United States Supreme Court broke faith with the American people and violated its duty under the Constitution. But we can change this lawlessness, and it begins by supporting our President, who respects the Constitution and the rule of law. Obama never did, but President Donald J. Trump does!

President Trump has made the appointment of a new generation of justices, in the philosophy of Justice Antonin Scalia, a strict constructionist of the Constitution, to serve on the United States Supreme Court, and the United States Senate will confirm them. It is imperative we replace the liberal activist justices like Ginsburg, Beyer, Kennedy, Sotomayor and Kagan with constitutional champions like Scalia, Thomas and Alito. The Roberts Court is a hotbed of judicial activists, and their alliance with the radical Left must be thwarted. The same must occur in our lower federal courts.

As we are all too aware, federal activist judges even now divine law to suit their political agenda, not what our Founders intended when they penned the Constitution. It is a perversion of the Law and a usurpation of the Constitution they took an oath to uphold.

Electing Donald Trump President and a Conservative Republican-led Congress is the means to preserving this constitutional republic and making America great again! We are half-way there, and We the People have much more work to do this day! After all, It's Morning Again in America!

The twelve Judges of the realm are as the twelve lions under Solomon's throne: they must be lions, but yet lions under the Throne.

~ Bacon, Speech, 1617, on the occasion of
Justice Hutton being sworn in as Judge of the Common Pleas

Chapter 11

The South

Any society which suppresses the heritage of its conquered minorities, prevents their history, and denies them their symbols, has sewn the seed of its own destruction.

~ William Wallace, 1281 A.D.

Everywhere we saw the Stars and Stripes, and everywhere we were told, half-laughingly, by grizzled ex-Confederates that they had never dreamed in the bygone days of bitterness to greet the old flag as they now were greeting it, and to send their sons, as now they were sending them, to fight and die under it.

~ President Theodore Roosevelt, 1899, recalling his march through the South, during the Spanish-American War, as a Lt. Col. in the "Rough Riders."

I love the South! It has given me many blessings. A home, friends, a place to live and work, a birthplace for my son, who was born in the bosom of the Deep South, at beautiful (yes, beautiful!) Fort Benning, Georgia, and a heritage!

The South is distinguished from virtually every other region of our great country. It is often referred to as the "Bible Belt," because of its deep Christian roots and family values. It is solidly conservative and Republican, and that fact was made abundantly clear in the 1980, '84, and, most recently, the 2000 presidential elections. The former elections were part of the Reagan landslides, and the latter voting in the South was key to President Bush's election! From a military and patriotic perspective, the South, per capita, has more American war heroes and Congressional Medal of Honor winners than any other region in the country. And chivalry continues to live in the South! It is a blessed land of faith, family, honor, tradition, and hope. But it did not become this way by mere chance. Our forefathers established this special region of America, and President Jefferson Davis and General Robert E. Lee must certainly be counted amongst those pivotal greats.

The South is vilified in the media for the Civil War and slavery, but such are the writings and reminiscing of the victors. The South was and is so much more! The South is foremost a region that held true -- and continues to hold true -- to the express words of the Constitution.

Today, we again find America on the brink of a new and even more costly Civil War. We find an overbearing federal government again usurping the Constitution, and broadening its powers beyond what the Founding Fathers ever designed it to have. Our Founding Fathers attempted to limit the thirst for power of that federal government by enacting the Tenth Amendment to the United States Constitution. And that Amendment, which is part of the Bill of Rights, was ratified on December 15, 1791. It stands for the proposition that we have a republic based on Federalism, which undergirds the entire plan of the original Constitution, by stating that the federal government possesses only those powers delegated to it by the states or the people.

In drafting this amendment, the framers had two purposes in mind: first, as a necessary rule of constructing how our government works; and second, as a reaffirmation of the nature of the federal system, but usurpers in the federal executive, legislative, and the judicial branches have substituted their wills for the fundamental laws and precepts upon which this great nation was founded. We see it in a federal government that ignores the laws of the land, and invades the very jurisdictions of the states to remove God and prayer from our classrooms and the public square, and dictates, amongst other things, the definition of "marriage," when "life" begins, and what constitutes "traditional families" and "states rights." It is a recipe for disaster. It divides the nation, and sets the stage for a coming secession, not unlike the one we experienced in the time of Davis and Lincoln.

As the President of the Confederate States of America, Jefferson Davis, prophetically warned, sixteen years after the Civil War formally ended, "The contest is not over, the strife is not ended. It has only entered upon a new and enlarged arena." His words have application to modern-day America.

But as for me, I am an American by birth, and a Southerner by choice and the good grace of God. I live in the Deep South, more precisely in the Great State of Georgia. It is my home. One can love their home state and the nation as well. Under our Constitution, it was meant to be that way! I believe all who dwell in freedom have a duty to preserve their heritage and protect their freedoms. This was my great motivation in writing this book. Protecting those things we love includes having the courage to speak out on the issues of our time, even if they are controversial. We must stand up for America and expose rumour and falsehoods to the bright light of Truth. As Winston Churchill once said, "Never give in, except to convictions of honor and good sense!"

Much occurred during my tenure as a Judge in the Great State of Georgia ~ including the 9-11 Attacks on America, the War on Terror, and the Afghan and Iraq Wars. These were events that required the action of good men to oppose the forces of evil that conspired to undermine and destroy a core set of values that can only be called, "American!" And there came with this challenge a resurgence of patriotism, but alas it was relatively short lived. Those forces of darkness successfully bided their time, and now pose an even greater threat to the survival of our Republic. Who would have believed only fourteen years, following the 9/11 attacks, there would be mosques being built across America in anticipation of the hordes of Muslim jihadist "refugees" Obama was welcoming into the heart of America. These immigrants do not assimilate, as Europe is discovering at this very moment. Add to that the fact Obama removed the worst of the Muslim terrorists from GITMO and shipped them back to the battlefield to potentially take more American lives.

And the removal of the symbols of our Southern Heritage and the memory of heroes like General Lee and President Davis from our nation's treasured past remains high on the agenda of America's enemies. For the past half-century, this politically correct, liberal mob finds no virtue in the past, only shame. And now they plot to remove all references to our Founding Fathers.

I am proud to say I joined other Americans in opposing these attacks on America's Founding Principles and core values. I love our country and believe in American Exceptionalism. On one winter's day in 2001 ~ on the 19th day of January, to be exact ~ I and many other Americans stood in the gap for our homeland. It was on the Birthday of General Robert E. Lee, and it occurred on the steps of historic Orange Hall in the picturesque City of St. Marys, distinguished as the Second Oldest City in the United States. It was a sunny, windy day in that coastal southern Georgia hamlet, and storm clouds were on the horizon. But Americans were gathered there. They included scores of patriots. Some young, some old, some black, some white, but all Americans, who, by birth or choice, took great pride in a culture and a set of values that identified them as Southerners. They all came to pay respects to the memory of a great American, General Robert E. Lee. He was called the "Southern Arthur," a noble king without a king's ambition, and a Washington without the reward of a man who was first in the hearts of his countrymen.

As you may have surmised, I consider General Lee a special man! Those who knew me throughout my military career will remember I often invoked the memory ~ and commented about the character and exploits of ~ General Lee, especially when my soldiers ~ and I ~ needed encouragement. Lee was such a figure to draw upon.

I was given a great honor on that day in Georgia, for I was invited to give the keynote address at this First and Historic celebration:

Remarks of the Honorable H.R. "Hal" Moroz at
A Birthday Celebration Honoring the Memory
of
General Robert E. Lee on January 19th 2001,
at Historic Orange Hall, St. Marys, Georgia

Ladies and Gentlemen, friends and fellow-countrymen, it is a distinct honor and privilege to stand before you today to honor the memory of a great American hero, a man who personified the virtues of Duty, Honor, and Country!

Indeed, it is an honor for me to be counted among the ranks of Americans such as you. Citizens who honor the memory of an American hero who placed service above self-interest, and gave us a Nation forged in Battle, and poised as no other in the History of Man. Robert E. Lee is a man worthy of recognition.

At a time in our history when men of courage and conviction were called into service for the South, Robert E. Lee stood as our champion, and he carried that mantle with great dignity, grace and humility. He was a son of the South, a native of Virginia, and always an American! A man who, like George Washington, answered his country's call to duty, and served with great distinction as a brilliant military leader. Lee, like Washington, was a founder and perpetuator of an ideal that independent-minded and freethinking men had dreamed of for thousands of years.

And Lee, like Washington before him, was unashamed to publicly seek the face of God. Robert E. Lee was the right man, at the right time, for the right cause.

Years ago, when I had the privilege to serve as an Army Officer, I commanded a unit in the 9th Infantry Regiment that had the dubious distinction in its long history of having met General Lee, the Army of Northern Virginia, and several Georgia brigades on one fateful day in May of 1863, in a little-known place called Chancellorsville. On that day, General Lee proved his mettle in Battle, and despite being heavily outnumbered, he outflanked the Union Army and dealt the Army of the Potomac a near-fatal blow. The Union Army quickly fled to the North. This was the military genius of Lee, but he was much more than a general.

His could have been a life of luxury, but Lee chose to take a stand, and when duty called, he always answered that call. Lee was a man of wealth and culture, but when the war had concluded, his home in Arlington was confiscated, its riches scattered, and he was reduced to living in a borrowed tenant house with his wife. His own misfortunes typified the fate of the Confederacy and the South. And through it all, he continued to deny himself as an example to his people. Lee's dignity and spirit of self-denial, rooted in his deep faith in God and Country, are fitting examples for us all. His life could be epitomized in one sentence from the Good Book he so often read: "If any man will come after me, let him deny himself, and take up his cross daily, and follow me."

On a rainy morning in October of 1870, as millions of Americans stood in hushed awe at the passing of this incredible man, one can only imagine what the multitudes were thinking. Some were no doubt recalling an incident just a brief moment before. A young mother had brought her baby to General Lee, asking him to bless her child. Lee, always a gentleman, carefully took the infant in his arms and said to the mother, "teach him he must deny himself." That is all.

Ladies and Gentlemen, I would like to think General Lee was not only speaking to that American, but he was speaking to us, and his words echo today like a clarion call to Glory.

Remember, a Birthday is also a time of celebration. If what I say touches a chord, please do not be afraid to applaud or cheer-and, although as a judge I rarely have people cheer or applaud in my courtroom, I personally have been known to get rather loud at Jaguars games during their many winning seasons! This is not a funeral, and, after all, General Lee was a man who enjoyed an enthusiastic audience!

With that said, I think it only fitting as we celebrate the Birthday of General Lee, we remember the sacrifice of all American patriots, and we extend our thanks to the organizers of today's event, Mr. Louis Register and all the Sons of Confederate Veterans gathered here today. Gentlemen, you honor the memories of our Founding Fathers!

These are citizens who have committed themselves to the proposition that our heritage as Southerners is a heritage of service and sacrifice, worthy of being honored as a national treasure, and without which this Nation could not survive and prosper. Robert E. Lee embodied that heritage, and mastered his moment in history.

It is often said that History repeats itself. Today, unfortunately, we live in a politically correct time ~ A time not unlike that which faced General Lee. A time when some would disregard the Constitution, dismantle the military and its traditions, and have contempt for the Rule of Law and those who champion its cause. A time of unprecedented attack on those family values and institutions that hold the very fabric of a civilized people together.

I know you are different. You believe in honor and tradition. You stand here today to honor the memory of a great American on his date of birth, and we stand under the flag of the Great State of Georgia—one of the last remaining symbols of a heritage worth preserving and defending, because, my friends, the virtues of duty, honor, and country are never out of style. Not here, not now, not ever!

The Flag of the Great State of Georgia—long may she fly over this land of the free and home of the brave!

When the first chapter of the history books opening the Twenty-first Century are written, it is my hope they will read: There once was a time in our Nation's history, when men and women of courage, citizens such as you, re-dedicated their lives to the vision of Robert E. Lee, and, in what would have been the final days of our Republic, changed the course of American history. You can do that!

Let it be said of us that we mastered our moment, that we held tight to the reigns of America's destiny, and we refused to forget those who sacrificed so much to give us this great land of Freedom and opportunity.

Ladies and Gentlemen, I stand before you humbled by the memory of General Lee and your recognition of him. Like you, I am blessed to be a citizen of this great Nation. An American by birth, and a Southerner by the Grace of God.

Thank you for this honor, and God Bless you all!

That was the speech, and such is the legacy of General Robert E. Lee: Citizen, Soldier, Hero, and Child of God! We should be so fortunate ... and blessed!

General Lee's fascinating life and legacy are an integral part of the American Spirit, woven in war with enduring lessons for us all. Love him or hate him, General Robert E. Lee redefined the American experience, and stands as a pivotal figure in the history of the Republic. His life and words deserve resurrecting, even if only to remind us of the enduring words of my Lord and Saviour, Jesus Christ, when He said, "if a house be divided against itself, that house cannot stand."[11]

General Lee knew those words, as He knew the Word of God and loved the Lord. So on that fateful spring day nearly 150 years ago, Union Gen. Ulysses S. Grant and Confederate Gen. Robert E. Lee met face to face in the parlor of Wilmer McLean's house in Appomattox Court House, Virginia. And on that historic occasion, on April 9, 1865, the two generals united as brothers under a common banner, and formalized the surrender of Lee's beloved Army of Northern Virginia, thus precipitating an end to four years of fighting between

---

[11] Mark 3:25. *Also see* Matthew 12:25 and Luke 11:17.

North and South. This act alone solidified a reunification that proved to be the foundation of a world power the likes of which never existed in the history of man. Not even Rome at her height could match the length and breathe of America's eventual ascendency in global influence and might.

So with this in mind, let each of us resurrect the Spirit of our Founding Fathers and their progeny, and in so doing highly resolve, as President Lincoln so appropriately observed in his Gettysburg address, "that this nation, under God, shall have a new birth of freedom -- and that government of the people, by the people, for the people, shall not perish from the earth."

And it was on that day in history at Appomattox Court House in the spring of 1865, after agreeing upon the terms of surrender, the two commanding generals, Robert E. Lee and Ulysses S. Grant, each selected three officers to oversee the surrender and parole of Lee's army. Later that day, Lee and six of his staff signed a document granting their parole.

On May 29, 1865, President Andrew Johnson issued a Proclamation of Amnesty and Pardon to persons who had participated in the rebellion against the United States. There were fourteen excepted classes, and members of those classes had to make special application to the President. General Lee was one of those classes.

General Lee sent an application to General Grant, and wrote the following to President Andrew Johnson on June 13, 1865:

Being excluded from the provisions of amnesty & pardon contained in the proclamation of the 29th Ulto; I hereby apply for the benefits, & full restoration of all rights & privileges extended to those included in its terms. I graduated at the Mil. Academy at West Point in June 1829. Resigned from the U.S. Army April '61. Was a General in the Confederate Army, & included in the surrender of the Army of N. Va. 9 April '65.

On October 2, 1865, the same day that Lee was inaugurated as president of Washington College in Lexington, Virginia, he signed his Amnesty Oath, thereby fully complying with the provisions of President Johnson's proclamation. But General Lee was not pardoned, nor was his citizenship restored. Secretary of State William H. Seward had given General Lee's application to a friend as a souvenir, and the State Department filed away the oath. Powerful forces in government sought to stain and delete the memory of this great and noble man from the pages of history, but their efforts were in vain ...

More than a hundred years later, in 1970, an archivist at the National Archives discovered General Lee's Amnesty Oath amongst State Department records.[12]

In 1975, Lee's full rights of citizenship were posthumously restored by a joint congressional resolution, signed into law by a Republican president, effective June 13, 1865. And at the

---

[12] General Records of the Department of State, RG 59.

August 5, 1975, signing ceremony, President Gerald R. Ford acknowledged the discovery of Lee's Oath of Allegiance in the National Archives and remarked:

> General Lee's character has been an example to succeeding generations, making the restoration of his citizenship an event in which every American can take pride.

So true! General Lee's character is an enduring example to us all! And the fact he was and is an American is something we who are blessed to call ourselves "Americans" can take great pride! General Robert E. Lee is an integral and enduring part of our heritage! He was a true American hero, our "Southern Arthur," a noble king without a king's ambition, and a Washington without the reward of a man who was first in the hearts of his countrymen. Lee was a special man!

His life and legacy and why the War was fought are something worth remembering and sharing with our children, perhaps even over the dinner table this very evening ... and in the days and years to come with future generations of Americans. Now that would be a very American thing to do!

It's Morning Again in America!

The contest is not over, the strife is not ended. It has only entered upon a new and enlarged arena.

~ President Jefferson Davis,
Confederate States of America
Address to the Mississippi Legislature
(16 years after the Civil War ended)

Chapter 12

The Purveyors of Political Correctness

The central task of education is virtue.

~ William J. Bennett,
Secretary of Education, Reagan Administration

History told us that most of America's major universities, including Harvard, Yale, Dartmouth, the University of Pennsylvania, and the others had been established by conservative Bible-believing Christians for the purpose of training servants for God. In our lifetimes we had watched too many denominational schools move from their original doctrinal positions to become something the founders did not have in mind.

~ Dr. Jerry Falwell,
Former Chancellor, Liberty University

I will start this chapter with an observation: Despite seven uninterrupted years of achieving every goal on their agenda, the Left in America is in a state of outrage! And that rage is most visible in the children of Obama we see protesting on college campuses in America, most notably the University of Missouri.

Barack Hussein Obama had success at every turn. Whether on ObamaCare, homosexual "marriage," increasing the minimum wage, increasing the national debt, enriching and empowering the fanatical Muslims in Iran and elsewhere, Obama received virtually no opposition from the Republican-led Congress or the Supreme Court. The high Court even violated its duty under the Constitution to support Obama's left-wing radical plan to socialize America's healthcare system.

But despite victory after victory, more Americans became unemployed, less people had adequate healthcare coverage, more were on food stamps and government assistance, and America became less secure and amassed more debt than ever before. Obama's victories were at the expense of America's livelihood and constitutional integrity. He instituted the philosophy of his Communist heroes and anti-American pastor under the guise of "Hope and Change," and the end result was bringing America to the brink of extinction as a global superpower and great force for good.

And what is the response of the selfish children of Obama when the Communist utopia our community organizer in chief promised came crashing down?

Well, they violently protest, of course, and they want to double down on the bankrupt policies. They, like the community organizer they worship, cry "racism" and demand even more radical change. These children of Obama want even more in taxes taken from hardworking American taxpayers to fund their foolishness. They even turn on the radical professors that taught them such anarchy and disrespect. They reap what they have sewn.

We see the violent protests of these children of Obama as they seek to thwart the Movement to Make America Great Again. They are the purveyors of anarchy.

America's college campuses are in chaos because of a numerical minority that aims to get their way, by force if necessary, and it has cascaded down through America's educational system. We are now raising a generation of idiots who know no better, because they were never taught properly in the first place. America must get back on track with extoling the virtues of a quality education, hard work, patriotism, Godliness, and selfless service!

Teaching for me has always been a source of enjoyment. The opportunity to directly affect the educational development of fellow Americans is an awesome responsibility, and it is one I have never taken lightly.

I began to formally teach college courses as an adjunct instructor with Central Texas College in 1984. At the time, I was an active duty Army officer, teaching on a part-time, evening basis. I taught American History and Government. Two subjects I have had a profound interest in since my youth. American History and Government—these two subjects have been much maligned in recent years. The latter for good cause, especially with the advent of the Obama era of a government-forced Common Core curriculum that has effectively re-written history.

Why not base our fundamental core curriculum in grade schools back to the "3 Rs" and the "C," that is, Reading, [W]riting, [A]rithmatic, and [Good] Citizenship? And then reinforce those concepts throughout life? They served us well during the Greatest Generation and years before. It worked for them and propelled America to societal and technological heights only dreamed of by mankind.

All too often, true American history, such as the significance of the Declaration of Independence and the Constitution, and with them men of character and integrity like Washington and Lee, and the impact they had on the shaping of the republic, has been erased from our children's history books and replaced with a politically correct philosophy that elevates men and women of questionable character and deeds. These are some of the Obama successes I observed earlier. We have replaced the observance of General Lee's birthday in January with a national holiday for a man who is far more worthy of a spot in the Clinton inner circle. Certainly we could have done better! Combine that with the wholesale vilification of our Founding Fathers, the Ten Commandments, and the Constitution in this new-age Common Core curriculum, and we wonder what has gone wrong with America's youth?

Obama used his Bully Pulpit to lead the charge to incite violence and contempt for our members of the law enforcement community. Not mincing words here, even that idiot mayor of Baltimore [and Secretary of the DNC] encouraged and empowered rioters in the Spring of 2015; as she shared with the press, "we also gave those who wished to destroy space to do that as well."[13] What kind of examples have we set for our nation's children?

Thankfully, President Trump will have none of that foolishness and lawlessness. His is a Movement that respects the Rule of Law and those who enforce it!

My frustration with the state of affairs in the world of academia began in my college years in the latter part of the 70's. The radical student protestors of the Vietnam War era in the 60's seemed to take refuge in the colleges and universities across America. For many of them, their college deferments kept them out of the war, and permanently out of the real world. Many became tenured professors in those schools and went on to foment their philosophies in the classrooms. Many

---

[13] Baltimore, MD, April 24, 2015 - Baltimore Mayor Stephanie Rawlings-Blake held a press conference to comment on the riots in honor of Freddie Gray, a citizen of Baltimore with a long criminal history. When a reporter asked her how Baltimore police would respond, she said she instructed the police officers to allow rioters to express themselves and that "we also gave those who wished to destroy space to do that as well."

never hid the fact that they loathed capitalism, the military, the police, and any semblance of authority. They were the flower children of the 60's, and they took great pleasure in their new platforms to protest the American establishment, that is, traditional family values, hard work, traditions of honor, and faith in God and country.

I never accepted the liberal, politically correct philosophy they espoused, and I took exception in the form of debate. In high school, I was a member of the Debate Team and learned to look at both sides of an issue before I took a side and argued based on the merits. My outspokenness rooted in facts and reason often cost me in the form of grades. In the world of academics, at least in some circles, innuendo and emotion were the order of the day. All in all, I was better for the experience, and learned without a doubt that one must be willing to understand the cause they support, and take a stand when it is challenged. I have learned to respect many points of view that are not necessarily my own, as long as they can be argued with facts and reason.

My experience as a professor in Massachusetts was particularly eye opening. That period started in the fall of 1987. I was just assigned by the Army to serve a tour of duty as an R.O.T.C. instructor. Specifically, I served as an Assistance Professor of Military Science at the University of Massachusetts in Amherst. I also taught R.O.T.C. classes at Western New England College in Springfield, Massachusetts. We had many fine students, but they were few and far between. The overwhelming student populations had apparently bought into the liberal mentality that presumed anything that had to do with the military was bad. The liberals were intolerant and bigoted, which was the epitome of what they called others who disagreed with their narrow points of view. They were the products of the overwhelmingly liberal faculty members that "educated" them.

I recall many occasions during that two-year assignment, which seemed like an eternity, when several professors of higher education liberally displayed utter contempt for American values and traditions, and, of course, the military, especially the U.S. Army.

I vividly recall on one occasion writing then-Secretary of Education William Bennett to voice my concern about the state of affairs on that campus. The Secretary was prompt and gracious in his response, reminding me very much of the man who obviously had a great influence on his life, President Reagan.

What was the Secretary's response? Be patient. Stay focused on the important things. Be an example for others to emulate. Don't be discouraged. And continue to fight the good fight. Give 'em hell! Words to live by. And so they were. And I did!

Thanks to the intervention of friends in the form of Lt. Col. Michael Hodson, from my earlier days at Fort Benning, and Maj. Gen. Robert Wagner, whom I had met at Fort Bragg, my tour of duty in what we called "the Peoples' Republic of Massachusetts" was cut short to just two years, and I was off to an assignment as an instructor on the General's Staff at Fort

Monroe, Virginia, on the magnificent Chesapeake Bay. My experience in Massachusetts made me appreciate a bumper sticker I once saw on a car along Interstate 95 on the Massachusetts-New Hampshire border. It read, "Live Free or Live in Massachusetts." That about sums it up. I have always had a soft spot in my heart for the State of New Hampshire and its citizens. What patriotic American couldn't help but love a state whose motto is "Live Free or Die"?

In later years, I would teach for a number of other institutions that took pride in the part they played in meeting America's higher education needs. I taught a wide variety of classes at the undergraduate and graduate levels, including Ethics in Business and Government, Decision Analysis, International Business, and Quantitative Methods. I found teaching as an adjunct Professor of Law at Florida Coastal School of Law in Jacksonville, Florida, particularly rewarding, both personally and professionally. Florida Coastal at the time was one of the newest ABA-accredited law schools in America, possessing a diverse and distinguished faculty committed to an imperative of civility that fosters decision-making on the basis of informed and reasoned judgment. I respect that!

But alas, as we have recently seen in the State of Missouri, a university president was forced to resign over allegations and threats by a small but vocal minority over unsubstantiated complaints, aided and abetted by liberal instructors and coaches. So much for the constitutional concept of due process. One instructor on the University of Missouri campus, an employee of the state no less, prohibited the freedom of the press and threatening mob violence against a student reporter. Not enough that this instructor was violating the Constitution or the rules of a civil society, this mob got their way. The inmates are running the asylums on many of America's college campuses. And they will reap what they sow.

In the interim, we should demand our representatives stop taxpayer funding of institutions like the University of Missouri and others that not only condone but enable the "Black Lives Matter" crowd to disrupt these campuses and interfere with the students who actually attend classes and want to make something of their lives. Defund these so-called "schools" of taxpayer funding, and see how fast the liberal instructors and community organizers wither on the vine.

Conservative Americans need to reassert themselves in these liberal hotbeds that were once designed to train America's future leaders. After all, it is the taxes taken from our hard-earned work that funds these places and provides the government-backed loans for these "students." No students who conduct themselves like the "students" we have seen on the Missouri and California campuses should be receiving taxpayer funding in any way, shape or form!

Throughout my adult life, I have always thought it important to participate in higher education. To challenge minds to excel and think "outside the box," and build a better nation for it. To share knowledge with others and, in the process, become a more learned person myself. There is a value to sharing real world experiences and a philosophy born of reason. God knows the youth of America get enough of the other side. I like to think of it as a fair and balanced education.

I often comment to friends that the young Liberal idiots we see today will eventually grow up, have responsibilities, pay taxes, and become Conservatives. But that seems less and less likely with the Democrat Party actively cultivating a base that is totally dependent on public welfare for their existence. This new poverty class in America will loyally support the candidate who promises the most government handouts. We see this in the popularity of Socialist Bernie Sanders and Hillary Clinton.

2 Thessalonians 3:10 states, "Now we command you, brethren, in the name of our Lord Jesus Christ, that ye withdraw yourselves from every brother that walketh disorderly, and not after the tradition which he received of us." Such Holy Scripture was universally embraced by our Founding Fathers!

In the words of Thomas Jefferson, "The democracy will cease to exist when you take away from those who are willing to work and give to those who would not."

It is little wonder why Jefferson and the rest of our Founders are hated by the Left. Obama has dedicated his presidency, and Hillary Clinton her political life, to eradicating the memory of these men and their Christian Founding Principles.

As this book goes to press, particularly concerning events are in progress. Even with the election of President Trump, institutionalized Liberal insurgents in the bureaucracy work to undermine our constitutionally-elected representatives. In our state and federal governments, they work to remove the likeness of our Founders and the phrase "In God We Trust" from our currency, and references to George Washington, Thomas Jefferson, and all our Founding Fathers are being replaced in the curriculum of young school children with politically correct historical figures.

The perpetrators of this political correctness that once cried for "tolerance," especially when it came to demands that we accept homosexual lifestyles as "natural," now expect the rest of America to abandon their rights. We see this in ridiculous homosexual "wedding cake" stories, where many in that movement are not content with obtaining these extra-societal "rights," they now want the traditional values to yield to their perversions. They demand the expulsion of God and the Holy Bible from our nation's classrooms, and, among other things, the acceptance and federal funding of the abortionists and baby part sellers.

The level of depravity on the part of the Left is sometimes hard to fathom, especially with its prevalence. They advocate so-called "art" that depicts the Cross of Christ in a jar of urine, while at the same time demanding punishment for anyone who would exercise their freedom of speech by drawing a picture of the so-called "Prophet" of Islam. And if the latter was done at any institution of higher learning, you can bet the "art" student and his or her instructors would be summarily dismissed, and the entire school population would undergo hours of so-called "sensitivity" training, which is more like indoctrination.

Nevertheless, those same perpetrators demand the silencing of any reference to the one true God, prayer, and traditional family values. Where is their call for tolerance now? Their hypocrisy is crystal clear and undeniably evident. This premeditated attack on America from within is most alarming, and it brings home the meaning of the words uttered by a dear friend in years gone by, the late William E. Simon, our former Secretary of the Treasury during the Nixon and Ford Administrations, when he said:

> On the eve of World War I, Sir Edward Grey, the British foreign secretary, issued a somber and prophetic warning. "The Lamps are going out," he said, "all over Europe." That statement could be repeated now, with one important, chilling difference. The lamps are going out, not simply on one continent, but all over the world...They are even in danger of going out in the United States — where the torch of liberty is supposed to burn its brightest.

I believe we were placed here at this moment in America's history to keep the torch of liberty burning bright, and to preserve and strengthen this last best hope for man on earth.

Is the education of our children important to you? Are your children in elementary or high school? Will your children soon be off to college? What will they learn? Who shall teach them? What path will they choose? Did you provide them the right guidance in their earlier years to help make them become discerning young adults? And can anything you say now help them on their walk through life?

I believe that those of us who are able to share wisdom with our youth have a duty to do so. Too neglect that duty exposes them to the pervasive and politically correct philosophy of the main stream media, their teachers, and the liberal politicians.

I am often blessed by individuals who me to share such wisdom, and I was honored by the pastor of a local church to share my thoughts about America in an address to Camden County High School's graduating Class of 2001. I was asked to be the Guest Speaker at the high school's baccalaureate ceremony, and it was an offer that I was more than happy to accept. I share this decade and a half old speech with you to demonstrate that some principles and values are never out of style ... and people long to hear the Truth!

Remarks of the Honorable H.R. "Hal" Moroz, Camden County High School Class of 2001 Baccalaureate Ceremony, First Baptist Church of St. Marys, Georgia, May 22nd, 2001

Ladies and gentlemen, distinguished honorees, friends, let me first say what an honor it is for me to be here with you tonight. I am humbled to stand before you. I believe this is a unique moment in our Nation's history, and a great time of opportunity.

Honored graduates, you have accomplished much, and I know I speak for all the good citizens of this county when I say, Congratulations, and Well Done! Tonight, you stand in the spotlight, and I would like to ask all gathered to recognize your achievement with a round of applause.

Would you join me? I would also like to recognize the ladies and gentlemen who supported tonight's graduates: The mothers, fathers, guardians, friends and relatives who made this event possible. So, too, would I like to recognize Pastor Keith Harwood [Pastor, First Baptist Church of St. Marys, Georgia] and Pastor Bob Moon [Pastor, Kingsland First United Methodist Church of Kingsland, Georgia]. Brother Keith and Brother Moon have a difficult task, as do all of our ministers of the Gospel. They stand in the gap for our communities. They boldly proclaim the truth, and they suffer the consequences for it.

My friends, it is not easy to take a stand, you make friends, but I dare say you make more enemies. Doing what's right is rarely easy, but it is something we are called to do. You and I. President Theodore Roosevelt once said, "Most people dwell in the Grey Twilight, which knows neither victory nor defeat."

Think about how true that is. I have heard it said that there are three kinds of people in the world. People who are oblivious to what goes on around them; People who hear about things that happen; And people who make things happen. Which one are you?

When Brother Keith first approached me about addressing you tonight, I thought, well, I can start off with a joke or other humorous line, and then get down to business. What I finally decided to do was not waste your time or the time of others in this audience. Time is precious, especially if you have a great deal to do. On the other hand, if you dwell in the Grey Twilight, time is really unimportant.

I believe you and I have a great deal to do, especially in the days and years ahead.

Tonight, I believe I am speaking to someone in this audience who may very well be a future President of the United States, a future pastor, a future legislator, judge, law enforcement officer, teacher, business leader, mother, father—you name it, each of whom has it within him or herself to change the course of American history for the better. How can I do that?—You might ask. How can one person make a difference in today's world?

226 years ago, Paul Revere entered the town of Lexington. It was around midnight. He had a message for the American people. An enemy was on the horizon: "The British are coming!" Later that morning, he was followed into town by 700 British soldiers. Regulars of the finest army the world had ever known to that point. They were met by 70 citizen-soldiers on the common. They were ordinary citizens, much like you and I. "Here once the embattled farmers stood," Emerson wrote, "and fired the shot heard round the world." They changed the course of American history!

Do you hear a call to action? A voice that cries out in the wilderness? Calling you to stand in the gap? Do you see things wrong in your lives, in our communities, in our state, and in our country? How will you answer that call? Will you close your eyes and ears to the evils of this day, and dwell in the Grey Twilight? I pray not!

Friends, we live in an interesting world. A politically correct world that tells us right is wrong and wrong is right. A world turned upside down, a world without absolutes, a world where anything goes, and you see it reflected on television, in our communities, and, yes, even in our government. You bear witness to that.

Last week, while he was being interviewed on the Fox News Network, CBS news anchorman Dan Rather said, I believe you can be honest and lie with great frequency (liberally paraphrasing his reference to former-President Clinton's integrity). Excuse me?

Two weeks ago, a New York school banned Mother's Day because it was thought to offend homosexual couples. What happened to tolerance in America? Do we now only tolerate Politically Correct ideas? What's next? Do we ban Memorial Day because it might offend anti-military activists? Do we ban 4th of July celebrations because it might offend those around the world who hate America and you and I because of what we stand for? Do we ban Labor Day because it might offend people on welfare? How about Thanksgiving and Christmas? Surely the concept of giving thanks to God and the name Jesus Christ offends people. When does the insanity end? And who among you would dare to draw a line, and say to those supporting this chaos, "Stop!"

As if that wasn't enough, today, we are told the only thing that separates us from a frog in a pond or a fish in the ocean is a hundred million years of evolution. I don't believe that! And I never will! Neither do I believe that you and I are here tonight by chance. I believe it was our destiny to be here! I believe that God in His own good pleasure had you and I here tonight for a purpose. I also believe it is not by mere chance that you and I are Americans. I also believe, as President Ronald Reagan believed, that America is separated from the rest of the world by two great oceans for a purpose! A fortress of hope in a lost world. I serve a God of order and purpose, who, despite what the Washington Post or The New York Times might say, is alive and well and has a plan for you!

I make no apologies for my admiration of President Ronald Reagan. I first met President Reagan in 1980, and one statement he made has been embedded in my mind ever since. He said, "With all the creative energy at our command, let us renew our faith and our hope — we have every right to dream heroic dreams." And so it is. President Reagan also said, "You and I have a rendezvous with destiny." And so we have.

My friends, I've read if you could shrink the earth's population down to 100 people, you would find: 57 would be Asians, 21 Europeans, 14 from North and South America, and 8 Africans; 52 would be female, 48 would be male; 70 would be non-Christian, 30 would be

Christians; 80 would live in substandard housing, 70 would be unable to read, 50 would suffer from malnutrition; 6 people would possess 59% of the world's wealth, and all 6 would be from the United States; And only 1 would have a college education. With that in mind, you and I are minorities in this world. In fact, we are a privileged super-minority! Much has been given to you, my friends, and I refuse to believe it was by mere chance. God intended it to be that way! The Bible says, "to whom much is given, much is expected." Much is expected of us.

Tonight, I step out of the Grey Twilight, and into the Sunshine! Will you join me?

Be careful! I warn you! When you take a stand for righteousness, when you stand in the gap, you risk making enemies. You also risk defeat, but you chance the opportunity for victory!

Last November 7th, my wife, Denise, and I voted at Mary Lee Clark Elementary school, here in St. Marys. We arrived to vote around 6:30pm, and waited on line until 8:45pm to finally vote. We were privileged to vote, and we did! Never did it cross my mind that hours later I would be called upon to become involved in the most controversial and historic election in our lifetimes, but I was.

I was asked to serve as a Presidential Ballot inspector in the State of Florida's recount process. I recognized there would be risks involved in supporting the Constitution and the candidate of my choice. "You can make enemies doing that," I was told!

In Florida, the Constitution of the United States was a topic of debate. I heard many, who should have known better, openly say, "It's out of date!" "It's a piece of paper holding 18th Century values — we're in the 21st Century for crying out loud!"

Make no mistake, my friends, the truth is: The Constitution is as important today as it ever was! President George Washington once said, "The cornerstones of our republic are the Bible and the Constitution." He was right, and the words of our Founding Father ring true today! You see, when you have nothing as a foundation, you are liable to fall for anything!

To those of you interested in a fair and balanced, behind the scenes look at post-election Florida, I commend to you a new book by Bill Sammon, titled, *At Any Cost*. I met Mr. Salmon in Florida, while he was a reporter for *The Washington Times*. He was amazed that those of us supporting the Bush candidacy were fighting for all military absentee ballots to be counted. Yes all! Even those who voted for Mr. Gore. Why? Because it was the right thing to do.

We should support our military personnel who dwell on the very edge of freedom's domain. They protect our liberties and our way of life. Mr. Sammon's book may open your eyes to many of the shenanigans by our friends on the left—acts that included ways to reject all legal election ballots cast by active duty military personnel. Again, the title is At Any Cost. I encourage you to read it!

Months after the election was finally decided, I overheard someone at the Courthouse say, "By what right did Bush become president?" And from a distance, I heard my friend, Chief Judge Harvey Fry say, "By the Constitution!" My friends, he was right!

Chief Magistrate Harvey Fry [Chief Magistrate, Camden County, Georgia]—when he asked me to serve with him on the Court, Judge Fry told me there were two requirements to doing the job well: Obey the Law and use common sense!

Now when have you heard advice like that in government? Obey the Law and use common sense! It sounds revolutionary today, doesn't it?

You and I are privileged to have that man's hand at the reigns when it comes to the administration of justice in our county. Do you agree? If so, let him know, and remember him when you cast your vote in the next election.

All of you honored here tonight will be old enough to do that by then. My friends, I challenge you to take a stand! Do what's right! Support people doing the right things, and oppose that which is evil. Take a step out of that Grey Twilight, and walk in the Sunshine!

How can I do that? By being a good citizen! Being good students, parents, teachers, law enforcement personnel, good workers — using your God-given talents to their maximum potential. Be that kind of person God intended you to be! Make great things happen! Never lose sight of right and wrong, and be not afraid to take a stand! President Andrew Jackson said, "One man of courage makes a majority." He was right!

Some here tonight might be thinking, Judge, that's easy for you to say! You're a judge, you're a lawyer. You can take a stand! It's no big deal if you lose! My friends, for the record, I grew up in poverty. My father died a month before President Kennedy was assassinated in 1963. Life was tough. You see, no one in my family ever completed college. Most did not graduate high school! I often heard from those in my community say that people like us were not meant to go to college. Maybe you have people like that in your community.

Well, as for me, I didn't believe those people, this is America! Where else could the son of a World War II Navy combat veteran, who grew up in poverty, dream great dreams and pursue them with any degree of success? The answer is simple: Only in America!

I count my blessings every day, and I always draw upon the words on an old chaplain I met during my many years of military service. He said, "trust in God, believe in yourself, and dare to dream!" You can do anything if you have faith! I often tell people interested in going to law school, "look, if I can do it, anyone can!" And so it is.

Here, tonight, you and I have the opportunity to commit ourselves to a great Quest. To change America for the better, and we can start by committing to improve ourselves for the better! Make us proud! Be the stuff of history! Make America a better place because of the positive influence you have on the people you meet and the institutions you touch! Some call such a

Quest following the Great Commission. And so it is!

My friends, I believe that when the first chapters of the history books opening the 21st Century are written, they will read: There once was a time in our Nation's history when men and women of courage, starting in this tiny hamlet in southern Georgia, stood in the gap for America, and in what would have been the final days of our republic, changed the course of American history. You can do that! Let it be said of us that we mastered our moment, that we held tight to the reigns of America's destiny, and we refused to settle for anything less than what our God-given talents could achieve.

But I also said leaving the comfort of the Grey Twilight runs the risk of defeat. And if we should fail, let future generations read of us: There once was a time in America's history when men and women of courage, took a stand for righteousness sake, and in the final days of our republic, never gave up the fight! My friends, we must never give up the fight!

Thank you for the honor of being here with you tonight. You make me proud to be an American! God bless each of you, and God bless America! Thank you!

What ever happened to Education in America? And what about the idea that patriotism and civility are actually good for our society? We have removed morality and God from our nation's classrooms, and we wonder why our classrooms are in such utter shambles!

The question is: When does the insanity stop?

The answer is twofold: (1) When responsible parents return to being involved in the education of their children, instead of some socialist bureaucrats in Washington; and (2) when we elect statesmen who will stop appointing champions of moral relativism and political correctness to elected office.

This is another reason why I wholeheartedly support the agenda of President Trump and our new Secretary of Education, Betsy DeVos. Both have set a bold vision for America's future that respects the foundation laid by our Founding Fathers. They understand the importance of the Constitution and an educational system that champions American values. They see an America that is exceptional and ready to be made great again!

The American people overwhelming reject the specious arguments of those who wish to expel God and prayers from our nation's schools and public forums. But for these judges who give life to these liberal notions that are diametrically opposed to our traditional values and heritage, we would be far better off. In the name of political correctness we have effectively undermined, and continue to undermine, those foundations which made this country great.

So, now more than ever, this is the time to support our President and those who will reverse the disastrous course America is on, and make our country great again! After all, we are Americans, and It's Morning Again in America!

Enter ye in at the strait gate: for wide is the gate, and broad is the way, that leadeth to destruction, and many there be which go in thereat:

Because strait is the gate, and narrow is the way, which leadeth unto life, and few there be that find it.

~ Matthew 7:13-14

Chapter 13

Profiles in Courage

One man of courage makes a majority.

~ President Andrew Jackson

Most people dwell in the Grey Twilight, which knows neither victory nor defeat. It is not the critic who counts, not the man who points out how the strong man stumbled or where the doer of deeds could have done better. The credit belongs to the man who is actually in the arena; whose face is marred by dust and sweat and blood; who strives valiantly; who errs and comes short again and again...who knows the great enthusiasm, the great devotions, and spends himself in a worthy cause; who at the least knows in the end the triumph of high achievement; and who, at the worst, if he fails, at least fails while doing greatly, so that his place shall never be with those cold and timid souls who know neither victory nor defeat.

~ President Theodore Roosevelt

Our Founding Fathers, despite what revisionist, politically correct historians may spout, were heroes, worthy of emulation, and I often think of them and their courage, especially during times of personal trial.

In that same tradition, no profile of courage would be complete if it failed to include our military and the law enforcement officers and firefighters. These are the men and women who provide the very blanket of freedom and security that allows us to live our lives as God intended. And many of these brave souls braved crumbling twin towers to rescue thousands of fellow-citizens in their time of need. They most genuinely reflect the words of Christ, when He said, "No man hath greater love than to lay down his life for a friend." Those policemen and firefighters, like the brave souls aboard the civilian jetliner that thwarted the hijacking attempt over the Pennsylvania countryside, a flight that may very well have targeted the White House or the Capitol on that fateful day of September 11, 2001, are truly American heroes. So too are the brave young Americans who answered the call to duty following the heinous attacks of the Muslim fanatics. They continue a tradition of service sparked by our Founding Fathers that has spanned wars in the desert, distant jungles, foreign shores, and here in our own homeland during the War Between the States and the Revolution.

As a youngster, and most certainly during our nation's Bicentennial Celebration, I often wondered what happened to the 56 men who signed the Declaration of Independence. My curiosity led to a dedicated research effort that revealed truly exceptional profiles of courage. These are profiles that we can all draw strength from. They are examples of great and enduring courage. They signed and they pledged their lives, their fortunes, and their sacred honour to a cause, an ideal that men had dreamed of for thousands of years. They forged a Declaration of Independence, which set forth the establishment of a nation apart from the Crown, through a revolution the likes of which was never seen in the history of man.

And true to their words, five signers of the Declaration of Independence were captured by the British as traitors, and tortured before they died. Nine of the 56 fought and died from wounds or hardships suffered during the Revolutionary War. Twelve had their homes ransacked and burned. Two lost their sons serving in the Continental Army, and two had sons captured.

But who were the Founding Fathers? Twenty-four were lawyers and jurists. Twelve were wealthy colonists of varied successful backgrounds. Eleven were merchants, and nine were farmers and large plantation owners. These were men of means, well educated, and they signed the Declaration of Independence knowing full well that the penalty would be death if they were captured. Carter Braxton of Virginia, a wealthy plantation owner and trader, saw his ships swept from the seas by the British Navy. He sold his home and properties to pay his debts, and he died a pauper. The British constantly pursued Thomas McKean of Delaware. His family lived as nomads during the Revolution, moving from one location to another, and always under cover of darkness and secrecy. He served in the Congress without pay, and his family was kept in hiding. His possessions were eventually taken from him, and poverty was his reward. Tories and British soldiers looted the properties of Ellery, Hall, Clymer, Walton, Gwinnett, Heyward, Rutledge, and Middleton. At the Battle of Yorktown, Thomas Nelson, Jr., noted that British General Cornwallis had taken over his family home as a headquarters. He quietly but firmly urged General George Washington to open fire. The home was destroyed, and Nelson eventually died bankrupt. Francis Lewis of New York had his home and properties destroyed. The enemy jailed his wife, and she died within a few months. John Hart of New Jersey was driven from his wife's bedside as she was dying. Their 13 children fled for their lives. His fields and his gristmill were laid to waste. For more than a year, he lived in forests and caves, returning home to find his wife dead and his children vanished. A few weeks later he died from exhaustion and a broken heart. Morris and Livingston, also from New Jersey, suffered similar fates. Such were the stories and sacrifices of the American Revolution. These were not selfish exploiters or opportunistic slave owners. They were soft-spoken men of means and education. They had security, but they valued liberty and their God-given rights more, and they were willing to step out of the Grey Twilight, and take a stand for future generations of Americans.

Make no mistake, the men who set their signatures to the Declaration of Independence understood that if things went wrong they would see their lives conclude most likely at the end of a rope on a scaffold. They were not profiteers seeking to expand their wealth. On the contrary, they were well educated, God-fearing freedom fighters, who knew no colony in the history of the British Empire ever declared its independence and successfully severed its ties with the Crown. More likely than not, their cause would fail, but these men chose death over a life without liberty. And the next time you look at a copy of the original Declaration of Independence, note John Hancock's signature. He signed his name extra-large, so that King George III could read it even without his spectacles. These men where truly profiles of courage!

Our Founding Fathers inspire me, and make me proud to be an American! It is my hope that after reading this book, you too have been inspired to develop a new sense of pride in our country and the principles it was founded on. The Founding Fathers defined what it means to be an "American." Their belief in God and His hand as a guiding force in the lives of men and nations is awe-inspiring!

The impact of our Founders echoes throughout the American landscape today, and I would be remiss if I did not acknowledge the ongoing work of friends like Donna Fiducia[14] and Don Neuen,[15] and Audrey Russo,[16] who like

---

[14] Donna Fiducia is a former anchor of Fox News Channel, NBC, CBS Radio, VH1, and current President of Donna Fiducia Productions and co-host of the Cowboy Logic Radio Show.

Paul Revere, sound the alarm against the forces of Political Correctness that are destroying our republic. They champion a return to the original intent of our Founding Fathers. And the selfless community work of spiritual leaders like Paul and Vickie Hafer. As the founders and leaders of the ministry staff at Lighthouse Christian Broadcasting, Paul and Vickie champion a Christian ministry ("The Lighthouse" WECC 89.3 FM, St. Marys, Georgia, & 105.9 FM, Waycross, Georgia, serving northeast Florida & southeast Georgia, & the world on the internet at TheLighthouseFM.org,) that shines His light on southeast Georgia and northeast Florida with a simple message of Truth and Life, providing the peace of Christ that surpasses all understanding. And they are not alone. Their ministry is part of a spiritual revival that can be found in hamlets throughout our great land. I have seen such revivals in lowly homes across America, where two or more are gathered in His name. They are the salt and light of our communities.

And I have witnessed great throngs in meeting places led by champions like the late Dr. Jerry Falwell in Virginia, and Dr. Charles Stanley in Atlanta. Each in their own right is fulfilling the Great Commission. These are the same kind of decent, God-loving citizens who filled the gap and provided Christian charity and brotherly love long before the federal and state governments ever dreamed of stepping in with their bloated welfare programs and affirmative action bureaucracies. Unlike the government programs, these

---

[15] Don Neuen is a businessman and the co-host of the Cowboy Logic Radio Show.
[16] Audrey Russo is the Host of the REEL Talk Radio Show, a columnist and radio commentator.

ministers of the Gospel nourish the body and the spirit, providing substance and meaning to life, not just a handout for living. Nevertheless, these people, by and large, are scorned by the politically correct crowd for their upright walk in life and strict adherence to the literal word of the Good Book. Their courage is self-evident! And they deserve our respect and they need our support!

This is particularly true of our Law Enforcement community! For the past eight years, they were held in contempt by the Obama regime. It is not a stretch to say that Barack Obama waged war on these brave men and women. I think of these American heroes who selflessly soldier on to protect our communities, regardless of the winds of political change. One such hero is Lt. Shannon Brock of the St. Marys Police Department in Georgia. I knew him when I served as a judge, and he was a patrolman … and I know him today! He is a leader in the law enforcement community, and stands between civilization and anarchy. I thank God for men and women such as these. I also think of Sheriff Jim Proctor and Major Chuck Byerly in Camden County, Georgia. These are the watchmen on the walls of this city on a hill that George Orwell eloquently mused about so many years ago:

"We sleep safe in our beds
because rough men stand ready in the night
to visit violence on those who would do us harm."

We meet profiles of courage every day. They walk among us. They work with us, and they work for us, and we work for them. You just have to know where to look! Many work in homes across America, mothers raising decent children despite great personal and financial hardship. Fathers working two jobs to provide a better future for their children. Visionaries pursuing their dreams, which we know as *"The American Dream."* Providing a better future for their children because of the contributions they make to their own communities. Some of these profiles of courage we will never see, because they walk lonely posts in far off lands on the very edge of freedom's domain. They are the men and women serving in our military, and they watch over us 24 hours a day!

These modern day profiles of courage are the progeny of those who gave birth to a nation, and an idea men had only dreamed of for thousands of years. I started this chapter with a tribute to our Founding Fathers, and I will end it that way.

This is their story. This is their legacy, one worth resurrecting and studying by this generation, and the generations of Americans to come.

It's Morning Again in America!

The leadership of men like Madison gave shape to a nation that would become the greatest the world has ever seen. Our Founding Fathers began the most exciting adventure in the history of nations. Their victory was to find a home for liberty.

~ President Ronald Reagan

Chapter 14

Why Not an Honest and Ethical Government?

Honesty in States, as well as Individuals will ever be found the soundest policy.

~ President George Washington,
November 5, 1787

Ethics as a subject is an interesting field of study. It is spoken about, written of, and taught in the most prestigious of our law and business schools and universities.

But what exactly are "Ethics?" I have taught Ethics in Business and Government as a university professor. I have defined Ethics as a sense of right and wrong, fairness and justice. It is a fascinating subject because ethical standards vary from one individual to another, one community to another, one culture to another, and so on. Even in our own society, ethical standards have changed over time. In years past, men of honor would resign their office if the mere appearance of impropriety in their conduct would taint the public's confidence in the high office they held, whatever that office was. Even lawyers are charged with avoiding so much as an appearance of impropriety, let alone a conflict of interest. President Nixon, for all of his faults, resigned to spare the country the divisive spectacle of its chief executive fighting partisan charges levelled by a Congress ruled by liberal Democrats. And the news media was certainly no friend of President Nixon. Even to the casual observer, in the eyes of the news media, Nixon was guilty until proven innocent. What ever happened to the constitutional right of due process in that instance?

In the recent past, we witnessed a chief executive by the name of Bill Clinton commit adultery, engage in sexual acts with an intern half his age and under his ultimate supervision, lie about the encounters to a national audience and a court of law, then besmirch the character of the young lady (and the many others who stepped forward to expose his repeated wrongdoing), then plead he made a mistake only after his activities were proved through scientific evidence (the famous stain on the dress) and fight like hell to keep his job, despite the fact he tainted the high office he held with his dishonorable conduct. His personal interests were placed above the country. But, in that instance, where was the cry of outrage from the news media? To them, Clinton was innocent even after the U.S. House of Representatives successfully voted to impeach him for his misconduct while in office. To them, no Clinton could do wrong, not Bill Clinton or his minister of propaganda in the White House, Hillary, who blamed his criminal indiscretions on "a vast right wing conspiracy!" Far be it a "leader" should take responsibility for his actions! An honorable man would have resigned before besmirching the high office of president, but that is not in the dubious nature of the Clintons.

More recently, we witnessed a chief executive engaged in a perpetual campaign to vilify America's law enforcement and military communities. Of course, I speak of Barack Hussein Obama, another dubious individual of questionable character and integrity. Obama has never been honest with the American people on the nature of his "fundamental transformation" of America. From Benghazi to his ObamaCare promises of "if you like your doctor, you can keep him," to the net result of his socialization of healthcare in America would result in the annual savings of many thousands of dollars by average families, Obama lied and his claims were false. And unfortunately, the Supreme Court aided this fraud by rewriting sections of the so-called "Affordable Healthcare Act" to aid him and violate their duty under the Constitution.

And when caught red-handed lying to the American people, Obama deflected the blame for his disastrous choices on his predecessor, George W. Bush. And when such a tactic proved less effective, he deferred to calling his detractors "racist!" His chorus in the Democrat Party continue that despicable practice with President Trump and we who support him. Again, far be it a "leader" should take responsibility for his actions. An honorable man would have resigned before besmirching the high office of president, but that too was not in the dubious nature of Barack Hussein Obama. But that does not dismiss the Republican-led Congress from having failed to fulfil its duty under the Constitution and file Articles of Impeachment against Obama for his high crimes and misdemeanors. Shame on those in the Congressional leadership at the time for not having done so!

Despite Clinton and Obama, I am here to say Ethics are important! There are the standards by which men and women of honor and integrity are expected to comport. This is a cornerstone of Western Civilization. Men and women of strong ethical character are in great demand, and they are the keys to our future. Our children need to understand this, and appreciate the virtues of ethical behavior, and the benefits of doing the often-difficult right thing over the easy wrong. In short, they need a moral compass, and they need a direction.

That's where parents come in—responsible parents—and good citizens willing to correct the misadventures of our youth—and those not so young! Years ago, when President Reagan was asked what he would have the American people do to solve the problems facing our society, he answered without hesitation, "If it were in my power, I'd have everyone obey the Ten Commandments and follow the Golden Rule."

The media elitists laughed off the president's response, but he was right! Without a code of ethics or a Code of Chivalry, and people to apply them, this country would be a jungle — uncivilized, violent and corrupt. The world is replete with such jungles — Somalia, Afghanistan, Iran, Iraq, and North Korea instantly spring to mind, but there are many more. Even in our own nation, we see the evidence of ethical breakdowns, and they appear in urban centers with corruption in government and the private sector, or when power failures occur, and neighbor turns against neighbor, and local businesses are looted. Our posh suburban communities are not immune from this ethical phenomenon either, especially when we see the disintegration of the traditional family unit and the proliferation of a drug culture and all of its consequences, one of which is the funding of the global networks of terror.

The current state of Ethics in Business and Government are a natural consequence of the ethical behavior found in us, as individuals, and our families, and our communities. They are also a reflection of our public figures, professional athletes and politicians. It is up to us, you and me, to change the ethical tone in America, and set an example for others to emulate.

Let us resolve to set the ethical standards for our time, and demand the same for our political leaders! Let us realize that this is the moment in history to rally around the banner of our ethical American heritage, right here and right now! That would be a major milestone toward making America great again!

It's Morning Again in America!

I pray Heaven bestow the best blessings on this House and all that shall hereafter inhabit it. May none but honest and wise men ever rule under this roof.

~ President John Adams,
At the Dedication of the White House,
November 2, 1800

Chapter 15

The Only Island of Freedom Left

Standing, as it were in the midst of falling empires, it should be our aim to assume a station and attitude, which will preserve us from being overwhelmed in their ruins.

~ President George Washington,
To the Secretary of War, December 13, 1798

We stand here on the only island of freedom that is left in the whole world. There is no place left to flee to...no place to escape to. We defend freedom here or it is gone. There is no place for us to run, only to make a stand. And if we fail, I think we face telling our children, and our children's children, what it was we found more precious than freedom. Because I am sure that someday — if we fail in this — there will be a generation that will ask.

~ President Ronald Reagan

President Reagan said, "We stand here on the only island of freedom that is left in the whole world." It is true! And that world is becoming smaller and more dangerous with each passing day!

International Law and Business are two fields of major interest to our government as we step out into the 21st Century. I taught the latter in universities, and I received a graduate education in the former at St. John's University in New York City. My experience in international diplomacy began at St. John's University's Graduate School of Politics and Government. I sat through many a class whose ranks included African and Middle East princes, royal family members, and would-be kings in distant lands. I often sat through diatribes of anti-American pontifications, and I often wondered why, if we were such an "evil imperialist power," they came to our shores for their education and the luxuries they so despised. Their mindset was in sync with Barack Obama and the students we have seen on our television screens at the University of Missouri. It was so hypocritical of them, and I never hesitated to tell them so. Many of the international students were here on student visas, and I often questioned the logic of allowing foreign radicals from terrorist-harboring, if not outright terrorist-sponsoring, nations to freely roam the United States and its great cities.

Unfortunately, my worst nightmares were realized two decades later with the acts of terrorism perpetrated on the United States and its citizens. And since 9-11, and more so under the Obama administration than any other, America is the target of Islam's rage. And Barack Hussein Obama has enabled the barbarians through his often open support for their cause, and his antagonistic approach to Christendom.

In the Trump Administration, we are restoring the rule of Law when it comes to America's immigration policies and practices. But President Trump needs our help and that of Congress to combat the activist liberal judges who seek to substitute their will for the Law. Foreign nationals from countries that harbor or sponsor terrorist activities should not be granted access to American soil. Nor should any culture like Islam, which refuses to assimilate into the melting pot which is America, be allowed to enter our safe harbor to destroy our way of life. Immigration to the United States, for whatever purpose, is a privilege, not a right. And foreign nationals, be they called "refugees" or "illegals" do not have a constitutional "right" to enter America! That is folly, and inconsistent with the laws established by Congress. President Trump has pledged to support the Constitution and protect America, and, God willing, he will!

I also question, then and now, the United Nations and its radical socialist, Muslim-embracing agenda, especially when it comes to condemning the United States and Israel on any number of issues. In college, my views were particularly troublesome to the students representing undemocratic nations on the African and Asian continents. They were also troubled when I questioned the newfound objective of the United Nations to become a supreme world government.

In a nutshell, the U.N. is anti-American hotbed for third-world despots. We should neither fund it nor have it contaminate our soil by being headquartered in America. We should defund it and remove it to a region of the world more suitable to its agenda, like Africa or the Islamic State-controlled area in the Middle East.

The truth is that the United Nations fostered, if not promoted, an atmosphere that made the 9-11 attacks on the United States possible. And recent oratory forays at the U.N. raise the specter of a U.N.-sanctioned global tax, designed to fund the United Nations and its questionable and, in many instances, un-American activities. And who do you suppose would pay the lion's share of that tax? The United States, of course! And by the Secretary's own calculations, the U.S. would pay some $100-plus billion a year in U.N. taxes. That, my friends, is ludicrous! Talk about taxation without representation!

The vast majority of U.N. members are uncivilized third-world states that have no business in a civilized forum, let alone being in a position to impose a tax or sanctions on other nations like a king would impose a tax or sanctions on his subjects. And that U.N. global tax initiative offends virtually all notions of American sovereignty and is ultimately counterproductive to American national security interests. The United States should have no part in that grab for power by a non-elected body of representatives from overwhelmingly undemocratic countries, who, by the way, are historically and consistently hostile to American interests. Foreign relations and business are important to the American economy and America's national security interests, but we must never compromise our national integrity for the sake of doing business with foreign governments for the sole purpose of creating a profit in the near term. This is why the "America First" policy heralded by President Trump is so vital to America's well-being and prosperity!

America stands for much more than wealth, it stands as a principled example of republican values, dedicated to the rights of men and the interests of freedom. These are more than mere words; they are a way of life. The tragic events of September 11th reminded Americans of what was and is at stake. Americans rallied around the President, the military, and Old Glory. We were willing to bear the burden, economically and emotionally, to support and defend those principles upon which this nation was founded. A free people, in the finest traditions of our Founding Fathers, rose to the occasion. And the fight goes on!

We must question the legitimacy of the United Nations, and what it has become, and what our future role should be with regard to that organization. It may have been established for a great and noble purpose, but it has deviated from that purpose. For years, even decades, it has served as a platform for radical nations to chastise the west, and condemn America and her allies for any variety of reasons. President Reagan recognized that fact, and suspended American payments to subsidize the very un-American activities of that institution, which is situated in New York City. It sent a message to the foreign diplomats who sat in the posh chairs that fill that place, a place where America had historically paid the lion's share of its budget. And it didn't take long for United Nations to change its tone, and I give you the Gulf War as an example of that change of attitude. The United Nations, uncharacteristically, actually supported the United States and our coalition allies in Desert Storm. However, that support disappeared with the advent of the Clinton years, and Iraq was allowed to continue her terrorism without so much as a whimper from the United Nations. Clinton also saw fit to hand over billions of American dollars to the United Nations, and continue payments to that institution which once again subsidized their very un-American activities. Obama only increased such payments to the U.N., and wound up actually supporting their radical agenda. Obama and the U.N. have much in common. It is my belief President Trump will change this!

International Business is, in its simplest form, conducted by a business across national borders. The business may operate in two or more countries. American businesses have gone international for a variety of reasons, the principle of which is profit. Profits are generated from gaining new markets and customers for the individual business' goods and/or services. There is nothing wrong with profit. Businesses that make money tend to pass that money on to their employees, who, in turn, spend, save and invest that money, and in the process build the economy and revenues for the government to provide essential services.

International Business tends to benefit all the countries it touches. It deserves noting that for American international businesses, the foreign nations we do business with need our presence more than we need them. In the final analysis, we must recognize this is a unique moment in American history and that of the world. No nation can withstand America's political or military power. Indeed, no group of nations in the Islamic world can withstand America's political or military power if we brought it to bear!

President Trump recognizes America's exceptionalism and potential for good! We have it within our awesome power to literally fulfill President Trump's inaugural address challenge to "unite the civilized world against radical Islamic terrorism, which we will eradicate completely from the face of the Earth." As President Reagan said a generation ago:

> We stand here on the only island of freedom that is left in the whole world. There is no place left to flee to…no place to escape to. We defend freedom here or it is gone. There is no place for us to run, only to make a stand. The line has been drawn.

We must repatriate American businesses that travelled outside of America because of the hostile tax policies imposed by Obama and others on their businesses. We must create incentives to grow America, our workforce, and our economic and military might! I believe Donald J. Trump has that vision, and the bold plans to make it so! Together, we can make America great again!

The terrorism that flourishes in the far off lands controlled by the Islamic State has already visited us in New York, Virginia and the Pennsylvania countryside. And there will no doubt be a great many more acts of terrorism perpetrated against American citizens on American soil before this is all done! Obama is sowing the seeds for such at this very moment, as he eases surveillance on domestic Muslim terrorist groups and invites the very worst of the Muslim jihadists who masquerade as "refugees" to our very homeland!

There is no place left to flee to, no place to escape to. We defend freedom here or it is gone. There is no place for us to run, only to make a stand.

At this moment in history, let us resolve, as a people — as Americans — to re-build America and boldly go forth and meet the enemy. Let us travel to distant shores and beyond, to repatriate American business and deal a death blow to our enemies, and let us defend freedom here before it is gone. We have the right to take arms, and the power meet justice, and the capacity to see it through — alone if we must, but we must!

It's Morning Again in America!

Today, our nation saw evil. None of us will ever forget this day, yet we go forward to defend freedom and all that is good and just in our world. Terrorist attacks can shake the foundations of our biggest buildings, but they cannot touch the foundation of America. These acts shatter steel, but they cannot dent the steel of American resolve. Those who make war against the United States have chosen their own destruction.

~ President George W. Bush,
September 11, 2001

Chapter 16

The Christmas Spirit

In spite of everything, we Americans are still uniquely blessed, not only with the rich bounty of our land but by a bounty of the spirit—a kind of year-round Christmas spirit that still makes our country a beacon of hope in a troubled world and that makes this Christmas and every Christmas even more special for all of us who number among our gifts the birthright of being an American.

~ President Ronald Reagan

The spirit of man is more important than mere physical strength, and the spiritual fiber of a nation than its wealth.

~ President Dwight D. Eisenhower

When I last visited the White House in the waning days of the first Bush Administration, in November or December of 1992, I departed that majestic, grand old house with a great sense of despair. An era was about to come to an end. President Reagan's Vice President was defeated in his bid for a second term as Chief Executive. The Reagan Era, for all intents and purposes, was over.

On that cold Washington day, I recalled with nostalgia eleven years prior, when the White House was decorated for Christmas, and President Reagan watched over a curious nation with an even more curious greeting for the public that holiday season. It seemed to hover over the cast iron gates that were the White House entrance gate along Pennsylvania Avenue, in a time before the Clinton Administration would seal off that street to vehicular traffic. It simply read: "Peace on Earth, Good Will Toward Friends." It was a take-off from the traditional passage in Luke 2-14, and it seemed to sum up the Reagan Administration, and America's rebirth in a post-Carter world. It was long overdue, and indescribably welcome!

But just what is the "Christmas Spirit" President Reagan so eloquently described in his speech quoted at the onset of this chapter?

It is a uniquely American Spirit, especially in a time we are all the more isolated in this very dangerous world. It is the spirit that prompts good Samaritans to enter burning and crumbling towers to save the lives of fellow citizens, strangers really, virtually all of whom they had never met before. It is the spirit that makes uncommon valor a common virtue.

But this Spirit has been lost since those days, especially with the Obama administration and its hostility toward Christians. Time and time again, Obama and his allies on the Left have vilified Christianity at every turn. Obama has defended the most extreme examples of Islam, and here I mean ISIS, but suggesting they are a natural by-product of the Crusades. "Christians," Obama said, "need to get down from their high horses!" Even one of the few contenders to Hillary Clinton's claim to the White House throne, Lincoln Chafee, proudly heralded his executive action banning the Christmas holiday from the Rhode Island calendar, as that state's former Governor. And I recall with sadness the Democratic National Convention booing the mention of God in 2012.

I am encouraged the President Donald J. Trump has pledged to welcome back Christmas in America. Not since Ronald Reagan have I heard a pledge to restore this treasured holy day in modern time! Well done, Mr. President!

The next time the Christmas shopping season visits us, take a moment. Stop and pause in the midst of the many, and realize how truly blessed we are as Americans to continue to celebrate a season to honor the birth of the Prince of Peace. A season with a spirit that allows us to share our love with others through the exchange of gifts, recognizing always the greatest gift bestowed upon man by God. And remember this unique and truly American Christmas Spirit is slowly vanishing across the face of the globe—a casualty of the politically correct armies at home and the Muslim fanatics abroad.

This Christmas Spirit rang loud and clear in the aftermath of the Japanese attack on Pearl Harbor and the September 11th attacks on America, and it is a spirit and a season that must not die! I sense it today in the Movement to Make America Great Again! It is a Spirit that unites us in a common cause, in an ethic that is part of the very foundation of our Republic!

President Trump promised in his campaign to renew the Christmas Spirit, and he did just that! And we must continue to do so with even greater vigor!

It's Morning Again in America!

So what ties us together? We're tied together by our belief in political democracy. We're tried together by our belief in religious freedom. We're tied together by our belief in capitalism, a free economy, where people make their own choices about the spending of their money. We're tied together because we respect human life. We're tied together because we respect the rule of law. Those are the group of ideas that make us Americans.

~ Mayor Rudolph Giuliani,
Mayor of the City of New York, December 27, 2001

Chapter 17

Deciding How to Make America Great Again

Hesitation and half measures lose all in war.

~ Napoleon

During my youth there were many wonderful sayings, now considered trite, that provided cryptic, yet prescient guidance for my life. Among them was one based on Luke 12:48: "To whom much is given of him much is required." Perhaps such sentiments are embarrassing in sophisticated company today, but I continue to believe this with all my heart. I do believe that we are required to wade into those things that matter to our country and our culture, no matter what the disincentives are, and no matter the personal cost. There is not one among us who wants to be set upon, or obligated to do and say difficult things. Yet, there is not one of us who could in good conscience stand by and watch a loved one or a defenseless person — or a vital national principle — perish alone, undefended, when our intervention could make all the difference. This may well be too dramatic an example. But nevertheless, put most simply: if we think that something is dreadfully wrong, then someone has to do something.

~ Justice Clarence Thomas, February 2001

In government, both at the local and national levels, the ability to learn from our mistakes and make better decisions is critical. Suffice it to say, no one has a monopoly on good decision making. I liken great decision makers to entrepreneurs, that is, their most prominent similarity is their willingness to take risks. A successful entrepreneur is called "lucky" by the average person, but I dare say that "luck" has little to do with it. A single success is almost always tempered by a great many failures. In the final analysis, the difference between a successful and an unsuccessful entrepreneur or statesman is learning from your mistakes, or, better yet, the mistakes of others.

Successful decision makers have learned how to make good decisions. And experience making particular kinds of decisions has a great deal to do with being a consistently good decision maker, provided, of course, we learn each and every time we make a decision.

I find these qualities in very few candidates for public office these days, but I do find them. Donald J. Trump, for example, was one such man. Far from perfect, he was a proven and successful leader and decision-maker. And when you combine that with his bold vision and plan to make America great again, he becomes the instrument to fulfil his campaign promise to Make America Great Again. Enough of us believed that to make him President and stem the tide of America's collapse. He is Our President!

I understand the hesitation some have in supporting President Trump. He is a political outsider. In many ways, so was Barack Hussein Obama, but Obama was unvetted, had no record of decision-making or experience that would lend itself to recognizing he had the ability or capacity to honor his promise to promote positive "Change" for our country. Obama was a community organizer. I still do not know what that means. But Obama had the support of the political Establishment and its propaganda arm in the mainstream media. Suffice it to say, the mainstream media of today -- and here I include the likes of "Fake News" purveyors like CNN, MSNBC, CBS, The New York Times, The Washington Post, NPR, etc., etc. -- in no way, shape or form represents "the press" our Founding Fathers envisioned when they wrote the Constitution.

Obama was a champion of globalism and the spokesman for a cabal that sought to erode America's moral and constitutional foundations. To a great extent, Obama was successful at that! Enough people were deceived by the promise of Obama that he would do right by America with his "Hope & Change" slogan, and they were wrong! And people expected "Change," but not the collapse of America's moral, military and economic standing in the world that he wrought.

Obama will go down in the annals of American history as the worst president in the history of the republic! But he earned that infamy with the help of a Congress and Supreme Court that aided and abetted him in his destructive agenda. And the mainstream media protected and championed the Obama agenda like no other. Obama is directly responsible for accumulating more national debt than all other American presidents combined. He divided America racially, and declared war on our law enforcement community. He used the Bully Pulpit in the most dishonorable of ways to promote America's downfall as a world power and force for good in the world.

But the question is how do we learn from our disastrous decision to elect someone like Barack Hussein Obama not once, but twice?

The answer lies in the process of decision making, which in its simplest form becomes a matter of problem solving. More often than not, unfortunately, I have seen the consequences of making poor decisions, then repeating the same poor decisions, only to compound the same old problem or create a new crisis.

Decision making in America is an art. Always has been. More than two centuries ago, Benjamin Franklin conveyed his method for making decisions of great consequence in a letter he addressed to a friend. And although the date was September 19, 1772, I assure you that the passage of time has done little to improve upon the dynamic for making sound decisions. It basically remains the same:

Dear Sir: In the affair of so much importance to you, wherein you ask my advice, I cannot, for want of sufficient premises, counsel you what to determine; but, if you please, I will tell you how. When those difficult cases occur, they are difficult chiefly because, while we have them under consideration, all the reasons pro and con are not present to the mind at the same time; but sometimes one set present themselves, and at other times another, the first being out of sight. Hence the various purposes or inclinations that alternatively prevail, and the uncertainty that perplexes us.

To get over this, my way is, to divide half a sheet of paper by a line into two columns, writing over the one pro, and over the other con; then, during three or four days' consideration, I put down under the different heads short hints of the different motives that at different times occur to me, for or against the measure.

When I have thus got them all together in one view, I endeavor to estimate their respective weights; and, where I find two (one on each side) that seem equal, I strike them both out. If I find a reason pro equal to some two reasons con, I strike out the three. If I judge some two reasons con equal to some three reasons pro, I strike out the five; and, thus proceeding, I find at length where the balance lies; and if, after a day or two of further consideration, nothing new that is of importance occurs on either side, I come to a determination accordingly. And, though the weight of reasons cannot be taken with the precision of algebraic qualities, yet, when each is thus considered separately and comparatively, and the whole lies before me, I think I can judge better, and am less liable to make a rash step; and in fact I have found great advantage from this kind of equation, in what may be called moral or prudential algebra.

Wishing sincerely that you may determine for the best, I am ever, my dear friend, yours, most affectionately, B. Franklin.

Benjamin Franklin was no lightweight in American history. He was a Founding Father and an international celebrity. He signed both the Declaration of Independence and the Constitution. In addition, he signed the Treaty of Alliance with France and the Peace Treaty with Britain that ultimately concluded the Revolutionary War. He is the only American to have his name of all four documents. He also proved lightning was electrical with his famous flying kite experiment in 1752, and later invented the lightning rod. Franklin published *Poor Richard's Almanack*, served as America's Postmaster, and even found time to serve as a Judge. He was a diplomat, statesman, inventor, and journalist. Franklin was a problem solver and a decision maker of the highest caliber.

In my own modest walk through life, I have developed a six-step process to make decisions. It is a technique I relate to students of business and law, and fellow champions of the Quest. It draws on the technique and wisdom of Franklin and others. Again, no one has a monopoly, but here goes: 1. Identify the Problem (or why the decision needs to be made). 2. Gather Information. 3. Develop Courses of Action (options to choose from). 4. Analyze the Courses of Action (weighing the pros and cons of each). 5. Implement Best Course of Action to Solve the Problem. 6. Evaluate the Outcome of Your Decision. That's it! And I dare say it is a logical way to address the problems that confront us in life, be they personal or political, business or pleasure.

There are many problems facing us as modern day leaders, not the least of which is too much information in this computer age, not enough time to get everything done, and not enough good choices to choose from to make a sound decision. We can change that, and my suggestions may help the process. We see many that follow a different regimen. Some are superior problem solvers, and have developed their own system. Others aimlessly walk, or perhaps stumble is a better word, through life, repeating the same old mistakes. The consequences are an American fabric torn and put asunder ~ broken families, marriages destroyed, instability in employment, a rejection of Biblical principles, cycle of crime, our community and national foundations eroded, and a consistent failure to meet goals or prosper. The good news is these too can be corrected. This is the essence of education and learning, and solving the problems of society.

The amazing dynamic of American decision-making is that it has been a relatively confined exercise. One person has a vision and makes a decision to pursue it. He sets a course based on that vision, and others follow. It is a dynamic that has unfolded countless times since the birth of our republic, when one man beheld the vision of a free and independent America, and others joined the Quest.

Today, Americans must make decisions on the future of America. Do we continue down this path of undermining the Christian heritage our nation was founded upon? Do we accept the decisions of the politically correct crowd that tell us prayer and Bible Study/Good Citizenship classes in public schools are "unconstitutional" because they violate their vision of a "separation between church and state?"

If the answer is Yes, then we must be prepared to live with the consequences. Consider this: If prayer in school and nativity scenes in the town square during Christmas become outlawed because government, so says the First Amendment to the Constitution, "shall make no law respecting an establishment of religion," what will be outlawed next?

Carry it to the next logical step. As I told my students of the law, one must examine the totality of the circumstances when we consider questions of the law. Surely then, if we remove God at one level, we must abolish the recognition of God in the halls of Congress and the Judiciary, on our currency, on official documents that identify "the year of our Lord," and so on. And what do we do with our houses of worship, our churches?

Do we stop having churches in incorporated cities because the local government must issue permits to these religious institutions, thus recognizing and respecting them as established religions? Or do we move the churches to unincorporated areas of the counties or states?

No, that won't work either, because they will still exist in the state! Should the IRS stop recognizing churches because it connotes respecting an establishment of religion? Perhaps the plan of the moral relativists and the politically correct crowd is to do away with the churches, the Christian church anyway, and any and all references to God — sounds like a throwback to the plans of Stalin and Castro in their heydays.

The decisions we must make do not end here. What about the security of America? And what about the internal state of affairs in America, as well as the events outside of our borders?

This, like no other time in our history, is a time for men of vision to make bold decisions and rally others to that cause. This is a time of great responsibility to be greatly borne, a time when we renew the promise of America. We know what the problems are, perhaps we have ignored them far too long, and we have gathered more than enough information.

I believe a thoughtful decision to make America great again demands a thorough follow-through. It was not enough to just elect Donald J. Trump President. We must follow-through with our support and finish the task! I have come to the conclusion that President Donald J. Trump is the best-suited and equipped leader to serve our nation as the messenger and the spokesman of the Movement and the Quest to make America great again! But he needs our continued support! President Trump needs a Conservative-Republican majority in Congress throughout his presidency. This is key to approving the next generation of Supreme Court justices to strictly adhere to the Constitution. We must re-establish the Rule of Law in America!

We have courses of action before us. This is our hour of action! We can accept the destiny that others have chosen for America -- a destiny of change from the sure foundations planted by our Founding Fathers -- or we can opt to oppose the enemies of America's heritage by challenging their limited successes.

Such change for the better can be registered with your tempered words of outrage at the rulings of the Left to your local radio, television and newspaper outlets. Social media outlets like Twitter and Facebook, as I discovered just within the past few years, are effective mediums for persuading politicians. Believe me, people out there are listening ... and you can influence more people than you know!

Congress can be persuaded to reign in those activist members of the judiciary by limiting their authority under the law. And President Trump is doing his best to seat judges and justices that will adhere to America's Founding Principles and the strict letter of the Constitution.

And in the meantime, you can support the initiatives of President Trump designed to make America great again, and opt to support the Bible-based teachings and activities of your local Christian radio stations and churches. But the most important thing you can do during this process is follow through, that is, once you have decided what you are going to do, to then get involved and make this nation and our communities better for it! Support and vote for candidates who will pledge to make America great again! Don't wait until it is too late! The time is NOW!

And it is always prudent to review your decisions. Make sure you made the right decisions. Often times candidates will make promises that they know they never intend to keep, like the politicians who promised to oppose the agenda of the Left, only to be given a majority in Congress and ultimately renege on those very promises. They are the very worst form of politicians, like Lindsey Graham, John McCain and John Kasich, just to name a few. We must hold our politicians accountable! President Trump is doing just that!

If you were a part of The Movement to Elect Donald Trump President, or a late bloomer, You can help solve the problems we face, and spread the word to others! We can change the course of American history for the better! Failure for America is not an option! The future of America is dependent on the decisions we make today!

Together, we can make America great again! It's Morning Again in America!

Be audacious and cunning in your plans, firm and persevering in their execution, determined to find a glorious end.

~ Clausewitz

Epilogue

Let's Make America Great Again

Let us raise a standard to which the wise and honest can repair; the rest is in the hands of God.

~ President George Washington,
from his Address to the Constitutional Convention, 1787

This story shall the good man teach his son; And Crispin Crispian shall ne'er go by, From this day to the ending of the world, But we in it shall be remembered, — We few, we happy few, we band of brothers; For he to-day that sheds his blood with me Shall be my brother; be he ne'er so vile, This day shall gentle his condition: And gentlemen in England now a-bed Shall think themselves accurs'd they were not here, And hold their manhoods cheap while any speaks That fought with us upon Saint Crispin's day.

~ Shakespeare, King Henry V, Act IV, Scene III

In the waning days of the British Empire, soldiers and knights sworn to the cause, before they departed on what could have very well been their final Quest, parted company with a simple saying: "I'll see you at sundown." They, better than most, knew that a cancer was spreading throughout the empire, and the day was fast approaching when men of honor would be left alone to stand in the gap. And one fateful day, just before the end, they would stand shoulder to shoulder in a last ditch effort to stem the tide, that is, to stop the sun from setting on that once-great institution, which contributed so greatly to the culture of Western Civilization, the British Empire.

Pax Americana is over! The peace we enjoyed has been squandered by a great many politicians. And here I blame not only Democrat Barack Hussein Obama, but the Republican-led Congress. They have forsaken their duty under the Constitution and their word to the American people to take a stand against the tyrannical regime that is the Obama Administration. Men like former Speaker John Boehner and Senate Majority Leader Mitch McConnell had their chance, and they blew it! It is now time for another generation of Americans, outsiders if you will, to enter the arena and repair the damage.

But it must be understood that an end the Pax Americana is not necessarily an end to America as a world superpower. The events that brought about an end to Greece and Rome and finally Great Britain as dominate world forces for good need not spell America's downfall. There is still time, but that precious time is dwindling.

America has many problems, but we have a great many more blessings. We have it within our power to avoid the fates that befell other great powers like Greece, Rome and Great Britain. We can change the course of American history! I believe that men and women of courage and good will can change the course of American history for the better. And in case you have any doubts, I am talking about YOU!

I believe in America! I believe God is the author of the American experience and our salvation. We are here not as the product of some evolutionary quirk of science, but as part of a great and divine plan to do good. We were perfectly placed here at this time in the history of the world to make a difference. I believe that too of President Donald J. Trump. He, like President Ronald Reagan and others before him in American history, can make America great again, but he cannot do it alone! It will take the concerned efforts of men and women to join this Movement, and propel America positively into the future.

But as I alluded to earlier, even as rich and as powerful as President Donald J. Trump may be, his message is infinitely greater! The power of the presidency rests not in wealth or personal power, it rests in the ability to positively influence others. That's called leadership! The President uses the Bully Pulpit to affect change by providing a vision for our citizens to rally around, and he appoints cabinet member to implement that vision, and he appoints members of the federal judiciary to uphold the strict letter of the Constitution regardless of what the other branches of government may say, or at least that is how it is supposed to be.

Barack Hussein Obama did not subscribe to that Founding Principle! He used the Bully Pulpit to divide America racially, politically and economically, and he used it as a platform to incite the lowest form of inhabitants in our land to riot and wage war against our law enforcement community. He also appointed lawyers to the federal judiciary that perverted the Constitution and made their will the law. This is Obama's legacy!

Nevertheless, we can fulfil President Reagan's vision that "America's best days are yet to come!" But it bears keeping in mind that there will be trials along the way. As the Good Book, particularly the Book of Psalms, proclaims, we learn more from our valley experiences than we do at the hilltops. My friends, we have spent the last eight years in the valley, let us rise to the occasion and march toward the top of the hill! The forces of darkness are great, but God is greater!

We must each in our own way labour to make America great again, adhering to our Christian Founding Principles, which are sewn in the very fabric our Declaration of Independence and the Constitution! As Psalm 127:1 states, "Except the LORD build the house, they labour in vain that build it: except the LORD keep the city, the watchman waketh but in vain." We need to rebuild America with a healthy reverence for our Creator and respect for the Rule of Law.

So there is no doubt, I lost my campaign for Congress in 1994, but the fight goes on. And I have come to realize that failure is sometimes the first step toward success. "Lay me down and bleed awhile," Reagan said in 1976. "Though I am wounded, I am not slain." As the Great Communicator said, "I shall rise and fight again."

This, my friends, is our time to rise and fight again! It is a defining moment in the history of our nation. Right here, right now, it begins—A time of great responsibility to be greatly borne. Let it be said of us that we mastered our moment, we kept what President Ronald Reagan called our "rendezvous with destiny," and we refused to let America go quietly into the night.

When the first chapter of the history books opening the 21st Century are written, let it be said of us—we happy few, we band of brothers, we last of the good knights—that we kept faith with our Founding Fathers, we stood in the gap, and, in what would have been the final days of our Republic, we never gave up the fight. We must never give up the fight!

My friends, Pax Americana is at an end. But unlike Rome and Great Britain, this does not necessarily mean the end of America's era as the preeminent force for good in the world. We have it within our power to break the cycle of history, but we must seize a vision of boldness for America future. We can reclaim the industrial base that fueled our economy and employed Americans, we can defend America's territorial integrity, build a great wall to our south, deport those who illegally violated our borders and exist here as criminals, rebuild our military and honor the Veterans who answered their country's call, especially our wounded warriors.

Do these themes sound familiar? They should. They are the bold vision of President Donald J. Trump. Now we must fight the good fight and make them a reality! We truly can make America great again!

This is the challenge of every American ... To take a stand for America! This is what it means to be an American, and what we are called to be. And I believe the thoughts and ideas I have articulated in this work were shared by our Founding Fathers and are still shared by the majority of Americans today, with implications that reach far beyond the bounds of personal self-interest.

I pray this work will be a wake-up call to the once Silent Majority, a call to action, and a source of hope and encouragement.

In 1775, Paul Revere entered the town of Lexington. It was around midnight, and he had a wake up message for the citizens: "The British are coming! The British are coming!"

The following morning, 700 British soldiers entered the town and were met by 70 citizen-soldiers on the Common. "Here once the embattled farmers stood," Emerson wrote, "and fired the shot heard round the world."

Today, we hear another call. A call to arms. We are at war on many fronts. A new kind of war against a global Muslim caliphate, and a war to confront an unprecedented attack against our children, our economy, our military, our sovereignty, and our cultural heritage. This is a war between the forces of good and evil for the survival of America and the last remnants of civilization. We cannot afford to lose!

If ever there was a time of need, a time for men and women of courage and good will to step forward and be counted, this is such a time: A time for you and I to stand in the gap for America and what remains of Western Civilization.

It is Morning Again in America under the administration of President Trump! This was no small achievement! However, it will take determination, effort, and a great resolve to succeed, but we can do it! We can make this last best hope for man on earth great again! Now that would be a very American thing to do! God willing, our goal will be achieved!

It's Morning Again in America!

If my people, which are called by my name, shall humble themselves, and pray, and seek my face, and turn from their wicked ways; then will I hear from heaven, and will forgive their sin, and will heal their land.

~ 2 Chronicles 7:14, KJV

About the Author

Judge Hal Moroz

Whether therefore ye eat, or drink, or whatsoever ye do,
do all to the glory of God.

~ Psalm 37:23

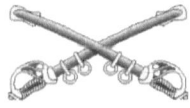

Hal Moroz is an Attorney and Counselor at Law, who served as a county judge and city chief judge in the great State of Georgia. His practice in the law has ranged from small city courts to the Supreme Court of the United States.

Judge Moroz is also an accomplished soldier and statesman, as well as a retired U.S. Army officer, having served in the Airborne Infantry. Judge Moroz served on the faculty of Florida Coastal School of Law in Jacksonville, Florida, and the State Bar of Georgia's Institute for Continuing Legal Education (ICLE) in the education of attorneys. He is a former candidate for the U.S. Congress, and served as Special Counsel to the Georgia Republican Party's First Congressional

District Committee in the 2000 primary and general elections, and went on to serve as a Presidential Ballot Inspector/Observer during the 2000 "recount" in Florida. Following the 2000 election, Judge Moroz was a candidate for federal judgeships in the U.S. District Court for the Middle District of Florida and the U.S. District Court for the Northern District of Illinois.

Hal Moroz is also a news and political commentator, sharing his insight of the law and politics on a variety of popular media programs. He is also a prolific writer, having authored numerous legal articles, weekly legal newspaper columns, and books. Copies of his many books can be ordered at Amazon.com or any major online bookstore!

Hal Moroz can be reached through an internet search
or through his email at: hal@morozlaw.com or his website:
MorozLaw.com

I am an American who lives in the shadow of the Cross ...

I walk humbly before God,
I stand tall before men,
And I stand in the gap for America!

~ Judge Hal Moroz

Obey God and leave all the consequences to Him!

~ Dr. Charles Stanley

Other Books by
Hal Moroz

- **America at Sunset**
- **Armor of the Republic**
- **Our Sons of The South**
- **Resurrecting Jefferson Davis**
- **Resurrecting Andrew Jackson**
- **Resurrecting Lee**
- **5 Things Every Veteran Needs to Know**
- **The Road Less Travelled**
- **Faith to Move Mountains**
- **Resurrecting Jesus**
- **Veterans Law & Benefits**
- **Re-Discovering Ronald Reagan**
- **Resurrecting Lincoln**
- **Resurrecting Kennedy**
- **Resurrecting Reagan**
- **Living a Godly Life**
- **Federal Benefits for Veterans, Dependents and Survivors**
- **President Ronald Reagan: Let's Make America Great Again!**
- **The New Knighthood**
- **A Christmas Carol** *(by Charles Dickens with a special Introduction by Hal Moroz)*
- **And Many More** *(Search for books by Hal Moroz at Amazon.com or any major online bookstore)*

ORDER YOUR COPIES TODAY!
And Order some as Gifts for Friends as well!

www.ingramcontent.com/pod-product-compliance
Lightning Source LLC
Chambersburg PA
CBHW030430290526
45786CB00001B/218